The Cripple of Inishmaan

The Cripple of Inishmaan is a strange and comic tale set on a remote island off the west coast of Ireland in 1934.

As word arrives on Inishmaan that the Hollywood director Robert Flaherty is coming to the neighbouring island of Inishmore to film *Man of Aran*, the one person who wants to be in the film more than anyone is young Cripple Billy, if only to break away from the tedium of his daily life.

Martin McDonagh's first play, *The Beauty Queen of Leenane*, a Druid/Royal Court co-production, opened in the New Town Hall Theatre, Galway, in February 1996 before playing at the Royal Court Theatre Upstairs in March. It won the 1996 Writers' Guild Award for the Best Fringe Play and was revived in November 1996 in the Royal Court's main house at the Duke of York's following an Irish tour. The play is the first in his Connemara Trilogy, the second and third (A Skull in Connemara and *The Lonesome West*) were premiered by Druid/Royal Court between June and September 1997. In 1996 Martin McDonagh won the George Devine Award and the *Evening Standard* Award for Most Promising Playwright, in 1997 *A Skull in Connemara* was nominated for an Olivier Award for Best New Comedy. He is resident playwright at the Royal National Theatre under the Pearson Television Writers' Scheme, where *The Cripple of Inishmaan* opened in January 1997.

THE CRIPPLE OF INISHMAAN

Martin McDonagh

Methuen Drama

A Methuen Modern Play

First published in Great Britain in 1997
by Methuen Drama

Methuen Publishing Limited
215 Vauxhall Bridge Road, London SW1V 1EJ

Peribo Pty Ltd, 58 Beaumont Road, Mount Kuring-Gai
NSW 2080, Australia, ACN 002 273 761
(for Australia and New Zealand)

10 9 8

ISBN 0 413 71590 6

A CIP catalogue record for this book is available from the
British Library

Papers used by Methuen Publishing Limited
are natural, recyclable products made from wood grown in
sustainable forests. The manufacturing processes conform to
the environmental regulations of the country of origin

Typeset by Wilmaset Ltd, Birkenhead, Wirral
Printed and bound in Great Britain by
Cox & Wyman Ltd, Reading, Berkshire

The Cripple of Inishmaan

The Cripple of Inishmaan was first performed in the Cottesloe auditorium of the Royal National Theatre on 12 December 1996. The cast was as follows:

Kate	Anita Reeves
Eileen	Dearbhla Molloy
Johnnypateenmike	Ray McBride
Billy	Ruaidhri Conroy
Bartley	Owen Sharpe
Helen	Aisling O'Sullivan
Babbybobby	Gary Lydon
Doctor	John Rogan
Mammy	Doreen Hepburn

Directed by Nicholas Hytner
Designed by Bob Crowley
Lighting by Mark Henderson
Music by Paddy Cunneen
Sound by Simon Baker

Characters

Kate, *mid sixties*.
Eileen, *mid sixties*.
Johnnypateenmike, *mid sixties*.
Billy, *seventeen/eighteen. Crippled*.
Bartley, *sixteen/seventeen*.
Helen, *seventeen/eighteen. Pretty*.
Babbybobby, *early thirties. Handsome, muscular*.
Doctor, *early forties*.
Mammy, *early nineties*.

Setting: The island of Inishmaan. 1934.

Scene One

A small country shop on the island of Inishmaan circa 1934. Door in right wall. Counter along back, behind which hang shelves of canned goods, mostly peas. An old dusty cloth sack hangs to the right of these, and to the left a doorway leads off to an unseen back room. A mirror hangs on the left wall and a table and chair are situated a few yards away from it. As the play begins, **Eileen Osbourne**, *late sixties, is placing some more cans onto the shelves. Her sister* **Kate** *enters from the back room.*

Kate   Is Billy not yet home?

Eileen   Not yet is Billy home.

Kate   I do worry awful about Billy when he's late returning home.

Eileen   I banged me arm on a can of peas worrying about Cripple Billy.

Kate   Was it your bad arm?

Eileen   No, it was me other arm.

Kate   It would have been worse if you'd banged your bad arm.

Eileen   It would have been worse, although it still hurt.

Kate   Now you have two bad arms.

Eileen   Well, I have one bad arm and one arm with a knock.

Kate   The knock will go away.

Eileen   The knock will go away.

Kate   And you'll be left with the one bad arm.

Eileen   The one bad arm will never go away.

Kate   Until the day you die.

Eileen   I should think about poor Billy, who has not only bad arms but bad legs too.

Kate   Billy has a host of troubles.

Eileen   Billy has a hundred troubles.

Kate   What time was this his appointment with McSharry was and his chest?

Eileen   I don't know what time.

Kate   I do worry awful about Billy when he's late in returning, d'you know?

Eileen   Already once you've said that sentence.

Kate   Am I not allowed to repeat me sentences so when I'm worried.

Eileen   You *are* allowed.

Kate (*pause*)   Billy may've fell down a hole with them feet of his.

Eileen   Billy has sense enough not to fall down holes, sure. That's more like something Bartley McCormick'd do is fall down holes.

Kate   Do you remember the time Bartley McCormick fell down the hole?

Eileen   Bartley McCormick's an awful thick.

Kate   He's either a thick or he doesn't look where he's going proper. (*Pause.*) Has the egg-man been?

Eileen   He has but he had no eggs.

Kate   A waste of time him coming, so.

Eileen   Well it was nice of him to come and not have us waiting for eggs that would never arrive.

Kate   If only Billy would pay us the same courtesy. Not with eggs but to come home quick and not have us worrying.

Eileen   Maybe Billy stopped to look at a cow like the other time.

Kate   A fool waste of time that is, looking at cows.

Eileen   If it makes him happy, sure, what harm? There are a hundred worse things to occupy a lad's time than cow-watching. Things would land him up in hell. Not just late for his tea.

Kate   Kissing lasses.

Eileen   Kissing lasses.

Kate (*pause*)   Ah, no chance of that with poor Billy.

Eileen   Poor Billy'll never be getting kissed. Unless it was be a blind girl.

Kate   A blind girl or a backward girl.

Eileen   Or Jim Finnegan's daughter.

Kate   She'd kiss anything.

Eileen   She'd kiss a bald donkey.

Kate   She'd kiss a bald donkey. And she'd still probably draw the line at Billy. Poor Billy.

Eileen   A shame too.

Kate   A shame too, because Billy does have a sweet face if you ignore the rest of him.

Eileen   Well he doesn't really.

Kate   He has a bit of a sweet face.

Eileen   Well he doesn't really, Kate.

Kate   Or his *eyes*, I'm saying. They're nice enough.

Eileen   Not being cruel to Billy but you'd see nicer eyes on a goat. If he had a nice personality you'd say all well and good, but all Billy has is he goes around staring at cows.

Kate   I'd like to ask him one day what good he gets, staring at cows.

Eileen   Staring at cows and reading books then.

Kate   No one'll ever marry him. We'll be stuck with him 'til the day we die.

Eileen   We will. (*Pause.*) I don't mind being stuck with him.

Kate   *I* don't mind being stuck with him. Billy's a good gosawer, despiting the cows.

Eileen   I hope that the news from McSharry was nothing to worry o'er.

Kate   I hope he gets home soon and not have us worrying. I do worry awful when Billy's late in returning.

The shop door opens and **Johnnypateenmike**, *an old man of about the same age of them, enters.*

Eileen   Johnnypateenmike.

Kate   Johnnypateen.

Johnny   How is all? Johnnypateenmike does have three pieces of news to be telling ye this day . . .

Kate   You didn't see Cripple Billy on your travels now, Johnnypateen?

Johnny   (*pause. Put out*)   You have interrupted me pieces of news now, Mrs Osbourne, and the third piece of news was a great piece of news, but if you want to interrupt me with fool questions so be it. Aye, I saw Cripple Billy on me travels. I saw him sitting on the hedgebank, the bottom of Darcy's fields.

Kate   What was he doing sitting on the hedgebank?

Johnny   Well what does he usually be doing? He was looking at a cow. Do ye have any more interruptions?

Kate   (*sadly*)   We don't.

Johnny   I will get on with me three pieces of news so. I will leave me best piece of news 'til the end so's you will be waiting for it. Me first piece of news, a fella o'er in Lettermore stole a book out of another fella's house and pegged it in the sea then.

Eileen   Sure that's no news at all, sure.

Johnny   I suppose it's not, now, only that the fella was the other fella's brother and the book he pegged was the *Holy Bible*! Eh?!

Kate   Lord save us!

Johnny Now is that no news at all?!

Eileen That *is* news, Johnnypateen, and big news.

Johnny I know well it's big news, and if I have any more doubting of how big me news is I'll be off on the road to somewhere me news is more appreciated.

Eileen Your news *is* appreciated, Johnnypateenmike.

Kate We never once doubted how big your news was, Johnnypateen.

Johnny Me second piece of news, Jack Ellery's goose bit Pat Brennan's cat on the tail and hurt that tail and Jack Ellery didn't even apologise for that goose's biting, and now Patty Brennan doesn't like Jack Ellery at all and Patty and Jack used to be great friends. Oh aye.

Eileen (*pause*) Is that the end of that piece of news?

Johnny That *is* the end of that piece of news.

Eileen Oh that's an awful big piece of news that is. Oh aye.

Eileen *rolls her eyes to the ceiling.*

Johnny That *is* an awful big piece of news. That goose might start a feud. I *hope* that goose does start a feud. I like a feud.

Kate I hope Patty and Jack do put it behind them and make up. Didn't they used walk hand-in-hand to school as ladeens?

Johnny *There's* a woman speaking if ever I heard one. What news is there in putting things behind ya? No news. You want a good feud, or at least a bible pegged about, or a thing like me third piece of news, which is about the biggest piece of news Johnnypateenmike has ever had . . .

Billy, *seventeen, one arm and one leg crippled, enters, shuffling.*

Billy I'm sorry I'm late, Aunty Kate and Aunty Eileen.

Johnny You've interrupted me news-telling, Cripple Billy.

Kate   What did the doctor say to you, Billy?

Billy   He said there was nothing on me chest at all but a bit of a wheeze and nothing but a bit of a wheeze.

Johnny   I didn't hear the lad had a wheeze. Why wasn't Johnnypateen informed?

Kate   Why are you so late home so, Billy? We was worried.

Billy   Oh I just had a sit-down for meself in the sun there at Darcy's fields.

Kate   A sit-down and did what?

Billy   A sit-down and did nothing.

Kate   Did nothing at all?

Billy   Did nothing at all.

Kate (*to* **Johnny**)   Now!

Billy   Nothing at all but look at a couple of cows came over to me.

Kate *turns away from him.*

Johnny (*to* **Kate**)   Now who's nowing?! Eh?!

Eileen   Can't you just leave cows alone, Billy?

Billy   I was just looking at them cows.

Johnny   Excuse me but wan't I talking . . . ?

Kate   There's nothing to see in cows! You're a grown man!

Billy   Well I *like* looking at a nice cow, and I won't let anybody tell me the differ.

Johnny (*screaming*)   Well if ye don't want to hear me news I'll take it and go! Talking about cows with a fecking eej!

Billy   A fecking eej, is it?

Eileen   Tell us your news, now, Johnnypateenmike.

Johnny   If ye've finished with the cow-talk I'll tell you me news, although I'm sure I'd get a better audience for it from fried winkles.

Kate   We're a good audience for it . . .

Eileen   We're a good audience for it . . .

Billy   Don't pander to him.

Johnny   Pander, is it, Cripple Billy?

Billy   And don't call me Cripple Billy, you.

Johnny   For why? Isn't your name Billy and aren't you a cripple?

Billy   Well do I go calling you 'Johnnypateenmike with the news that's so boring it'd bore the head off a dead bee'?

Johnny   Boring is it? How is this for boring news so . . .

Billy   At least you do agree it's boring news anyways. That's one thing.

Johnny (*pause*)   From Hollywood, California, in America they're coming, led be a Yank be the name of Robert Flaherty, one of the most famous and richest Yanks there is. Coming there to Inishmore they're coming and why are they coming? I'll tell you why they're coming. To go making a moving picture film will cost o'er a million dollars, will be shown throughout the world, will show life how it's lived on the islands, will make film stars of whosoever should be chose to take part in it and will take them back to Hollywood then and be giving them a life free of work, or anyways only acting work which couldn't be called work at all, it's only talking. Colman King I know already they've chosen for a role, and a hundred dollars a week he's on, and if Colman King can play a role in a film anybody can play a role in a film, for Colman King is as ugly as a brick of baked shite and everybody agrees, and excuse me language but I'm only being descriptive. A little exodus Johnnypateenmike foresees to the big island so, of any lasses or lads in these parts with the looks of a film star about them, wants to make their mark in America. That rules out all in this household, I know, it goes without saying, unless of course it's cripples and ingrates they're looking for. Me in me younger days they'd've been sure to've took, what with me blue eyes and me fine head of hair, and probably still today they'd be after taking me, what with me fine oratory skills could outdo any beggar the Dublin stage, only, as ye know, I have me drunkard mammy to look after. 'The Man of Aran' they're going calling the film, and Ireland mustn't be such a bad place so if the Yanks want to come to Ireland to do their filming.

Billy *sits on the side-table, deep in thought.*

Johnny   That was Johnnypateen's third piece of news, and I'll ask you now, bad-leg-boy, if that was a boring piece of news?

Billy   That wasn't nearly a boring piece of news. That was the biggest piece of news I did ever hear.

Johnny   Well if we've agreed on the bigness of me news . . . 'Bigness' isn't a word, I know, but I can't be bothered to think of a better one for the likes of ye . . . I will take me payment in kind for that piece of news, and me payment today will be a small boxeen of eggs for I do fancy an omelette, I do.

Eileen   Oh.

Billy   What 'oh'?

Eileen   The egg-man came and he had no eggs.

Johnny   No eggs?! I've gave you me big piece of news on top of me two smaller but almost as good pieces of news and ye've no eggs?!

Eileen   He said the hens weren't laying and Slippy Helen dropped the only eggs he had.

Johnny   What do ye have for me tea so?

Eileen   We've peas.

Johnny   Peas! Sure peas won't go far for a grown man's tea. Give me that bit of bacon there, so. That one there.

Eileen   Which one? The lean one?

Johnny   The lean one, aye.

Eileen Jeez, your news wasn't *that* bloody big, Johnnypateen.

Johnny *stares at them hatefully, then exits, fuming.*

Eileen That fella.

Kate We oughtn't be getting on his wrong side, now, Eileen. How else will we know what's going on in the outside world but for Johnny?

Eileen But isn't that the first decent bit of news that fella's had in twenty years?

Kate Aye, and we might miss out on the next bit, now.

Eileen Coming with his egg extortions every week.

Billy That was an interesting bit of news, aye.

Kate (*approaching him*) You're not usually at all interested in Johnnypat's biteens of news, Billy.

Billy Not when they're about frogs falling over, no. When they're about films and getting away from Inishmaan I am, aye.

Kate You're not thinking about your poor mammy and daddy again, are ya?

Billy No, now. I'm just thinking about general things for meself, now.

Eileen Is he off again?

Kate (*sighing*) He is.

Eileen Off thinking?

Kate That lad'll never be told.

Eileen The doctor didn't look at your head when he looked at your chest did he, Billy?

Billy (*blankly*) No.

Eileen I think that's the next thing to go checking out is his head.

Kate I think that's the next item on the agenda, aye.

The shop door bangs open. **Johnny** *sticks his head in.*

Johnny (*angrily*)   If ye aren't chasing after me I'll take your bloody peas, so!

Eileen *hands* **Johnny** *a can of peas.* **Johnny** *slams the door on his exit,* **Billy** *not noticing him at all, the women bemused. Blackout.*

Scene Two

Bartley, *sixteen, at the counter, looking over the penny-sweets in the two rectangular boxes* **Eileen** *is tilting up for him.* **Billy** *is sitting on the chair, reading.*

Bartley (*pause*)   Do ya have any Mintios?

Eileen   We have only what you see, Bartley McCormick.

Bartley   In America they do have Mintios.

Eileen   Go to America so.

Bartley   Me Aunty Mary did send me seven Mintios in a package.

Eileen   Good on your Aunty Mary.

Bartley   From Boston Massachusetts.

Eileen   From Boston Massachusetts, uh-huh.

Bartley   But you have none?

Eileen   We have only what you see.

Bartley   You should get some Mintios really, because Mintios are nice sweeties. You should order some in. You should get somebody from America to go sending you some. In a package. Now I'll have to be taking another look for meself.

Eileen   Take another look for yourself, aye.

Bartley *looks over the boxes again.* **Billy** *smiles at* **Eileen**, *who rolls her eyes to the ceiling and smiles back.*

Bartley (*pause*)   Do ya have any Yalla-mallows?

Eileen (*pause*)   We have only what you see.

Bartley   They do have Yalla-mallows in America.

Eileen   Oh aye. I suppose your Aunty Mary did send you some in a package.

Bartley   No. She sent me a photograph of some in a package. The only proper sweeties she sent me were the seven Mintios. (*Pause.*) Really it would've been better if she'd only sent me *four* Mintios, and then put in three Yalla-mallows with them, so then I could've had like a selection. Or three Mintios and four Yalla-mallows. Aye. But, ah, I was happy enough with the seven Mintios if truth be told. Mintios are nice sweeties. Although the photograph of the Yalla-mallows did raise me curiosity about them. (*Pause.*) But you have none?

Eileen   Yalla-mallows?

Bartley   Eye.

Eileen   No.

Bartley   Oh.

Eileen   We have only what you see.

Bartley   I'll have to be taking another look for meself so. I want something to go sucking on. For the trip, y'know?

Billy   For what trip, Bartley?

The shop door bangs open and **Helen**, *a pretty girl of about seventeen, enters, shouting at* **Bartley**.

Helen   Are you fecking coming, you, fecker?!

Bartley   I'm picking me sweeties.

Helen   Oh you and your fecking sweeties!

Eileen   Lasses swearing, now!

Helen   Lasses swearing, aye, and why shouldn't lasses be swearing when it's an hour for their eejit fecking brother it is they're kept waiting. Hello, Cripple Billy.

Billy   Hello there, Helen.

Helen   Is it another oul book you're going reading?

Billy   It is.

Helen   You never stop, do ya?

Billy   I don't. Or, I do *sometimes* stop . . .

Eileen   I heard you did drop all the eggs on the egg-man the other day, Helen, broke the lot of them.

Helen   I didn't drop them eggs at all. I went pegging them at Father Barratt, got him bang in the gob with fecking four of them.

Eileen   You went pegging them at Father Barratt?

Helen   I did. Are you repeating me now, Mrs?

Eileen   Sure, pegging eggs at a priest, isn't it pure against God?

Helen   Oh, maybe it is, but if God went touching me arse in choir practice I'd peg eggs at that fecker too.

Eileen   Father Barratt went touching your . . . behind in choir pr . .

Helen   Not me behind, no. Me *arse*, Mrs. Me *arse*.

Eileen   I don't believe you at all, Helen McCormick.

Helen   And what the feck d'you think I care what you believe?

Billy   Helen, now . . .

Bartley   The worst part of the entire affair, it was a sheer waste of eggs, because I do like a nice egg, I do, oh aye.

Helen   Are you entering the egg debate or are you buying your fecking sweeties, you?

Bartley (*to* **Eileen**)   Do you have any Chocky-top Drops, Mrs?

Eileen (*pause*)   You know what me answer's going to be, don't you, Bartley?

Bartley   Your answer's going to be ye have only what I see.

Eileen   We're getting somewhere now.

Bartley   I'll take another look for meself, so.

Helen *sighs, idles over to* **Billy**, *takes his book from him, looks at its cover, grimaces and gives it back.*

Billy   Are ye going on a trip, did Bartley say?

Helen   We're sailing o'er to Inishmore to be in this film they're filming.

Bartley   Ireland mustn't be such a bad place, so, if the Yanks want to come here to do their filming.

Helen   From the entire of the world they chose Ireland, sure.

Bartley   There's a French fella living in Rosmuck nowadays, d'you know?

Eileen   Is there?

Bartley   What's this, now, that the French fella does do, Helen? Wasn't it some funny thing?

Helen   Dentist.

Bartley   Dentist. He goes around speaking French at people too, and everybody just laughs at him. Behind his back, like, y'know?

Helen   Ireland mustn't be such a bad place if French fellas want to live in Ireland.

Billy   When is it you're going, so, Helen, to the filming?

Helen   The morning-tide tomorrow we're going.

Bartley   I can't wait to go acting in the film.

Helen   You, are you picking or are you talking?

Bartley   I'm picking *and* talking.

Helen   You'll be picking, talking and having your bollocks kicked for ya if ya back-talk me again, ya feck.

Bartley   Oh aye.

Billy   Sure, why would you think they'd let you be in the filming at all, Helen?

Helen   Sure, look at as pretty as I am. If I'm pretty enough to get clergymen groping me arse, it won't be too hard to wrap film fellas round me fingers.

Bartley   Sure, getting clergymen groping your arse doesn't take much skill. It isn't being pretty they go for. It's more being on your own and small.

Helen   If it's being on your own and small, why so has Cripple Billy never had his arse groped be priests?

Bartley   You don't know at all Cripple Billy's never had his arse groped be priests.

Helen   Have you ever had your arse groped be priests, Cripple Billy?

Billy   No.

Helen   *Now.*

Bartley   I suppose they have to draw the line somewhere.

Helen   And you, you're small and often on your own. Have you ever had your arse groped be priests?

Bartley (*quietly*)   Not me arse, no.

Helen   D'ya see?

Bartley (*to* **Eileen**)   Do ya have any Fripple-Frapples, Mrs?

Eileen *stares at him, puts the boxes down on the counter and exits into the back room.*

Bartley   Where are you going, Mrs? What about me sweeties, Mrs?

Helen   You've done it now, haven't ya?

Bartley   Your oul aunty's a mad woman, Cripple Billy.

Helen   Mrs Osbourne isn't Cripple Billy's aunty at all, anyways. She's only his pretend aunty, same as the other one. Isn't that right, Billy?

Billy   It is.

Helen   They only took him in when Billy's mam and dad went and drowned themselves, when they found out Billy was born a cripple-boy.

Billy   They didn't go and drowned themselves.

Helen   Oh aye, aye . . .

Billy   They only fell o'erboard in rough seas.

Helen   Uh-huh. What were they doing sailing in rough seas, so, and wasn't it at night-time too?

Billy   Trying to get to America be the mainland they were.

Helen   No, trying to get away from you they were, be distance or be death, it made no differ to them.

Billy   Well how the hell would you know when you were just a babby at the time, the same as me?

Helen   I gave Johnnypateen a cheesy praitie one time and he told me. Wasn't it him was left there holding ya, down be the waterside?

Billy   Well what did he know was in their heads that night? He wasn't in that boat.

Helen   Sure didn't they have a sackful of stones tied between themselves?

Billy   That's pure gossip that they had a sackful of stones tied between themselves, and even Johnnypateen agrees on that one . . .

Bartley   Maybe he had a telescope.

Helen (*pause*)   Maybe who had a telescope?

Bartley   Maybe Johnnypateenmike had a telescope.

Helen   What differ would having a telescope have?

Bartley *thinks, then shrugs.*

Helen   You and your fecking telescopes. You're always throwing telescopes into the fecking conversation.

Bartley   They do have a great array of telescopes in America now, d'know? You can see a worm a mile away.

Helen   Why would you want to see a worm a mile away?

Bartley   To see what he was up to.

Helen   What do worms usually be up to?

Bartley   Wriggling.

Helen   Wriggling. And how much do telescopes cost?

Bartley   Twelve dollars for a good one.

Helen   So you'd pay twelve dollars to find out worms go wriggling?

Bartley (*pause*)   *Aye*. I would.

Helen   You don't have twelve hairs on your bollocks, let alone twelve dollars.

Bartley   I don't have twelve dollars on me bollocks, no, you're right there. I saw no sense.

Helen *approaches him.*

Bartley   Don't, Helen . . .

Helen *punches him hard in the stomach.*

Bartley (*winded*)   Hurt me ribs that punch did.

Helen   Feck your ribs. Using that kind of fecking language to me, eh? (*Pause.*) What was we talking about, Cripple Billy? Oh eye, your dead mammy and daddy.

Billy   They didn't go drowning themselves because of me. They loved me.

Helen   They loved you? Would *you* love you if you weren't you? You barely love you and you *are* you.

Bartley (*winded*)   At least Cripple Billy doesn't punch poor lads' ribs for them.

Helen   No, and why? Because he's too fecking feeble to. It'd feel like a punch from a wet goose.

Bartley (*excited*)   Did ye hear Jack Ellery's goose bit Patty Brennan's cat on the tail and hurt that tail . . .

Helen   We *did* hear.

Bartley   Oh. (*Pause.*) And Jack didn't even apologise for that goose's biting and now Patty Brennan . . .

Helen   Didn't I just say we fecking heard, sure?

Bartley   I thought Billy mightn't have heard.

Helen   Sure Billy's busy thinking about his drowned mammy and daddy, Bartley. He doesn't need any of your days-old goose-news. Aren't you thinking about your drowned mammy and daddy, Billy?

Billy   I am.

Helen   You've never been on the sea since the day they died, have you, Billy? Aren't you too scared?

Billy   I *am* too scared.

Helen   What a big sissy-arse, eh, Bartley?

Bartley   Sure anybody with a brain is at least a biteen afraid of the sea.

Helen   *I'm* not a biteen afraid of the sea.

Bartley   Well there you go, now.

Billy *laughs*.

Helen   Eh? Was that an insult?!

Bartley   How would that be an insult, saying you're not afraid of the sea?

Helen   Why did Cripple Billy laugh so?

Bartley   Cripple Billy only laughed cos he's an odd boy. Isn't that right, Cripple Billy?

Billy   It is, aye. Oh plain odd I am.

Helen *pauses, confused*.

Bartley   Is it true you got nigh on a hundred pounds insurance when your mammy and daddy drowned, Billy?

Billy   It is.

Bartley   Jeebies. Do ya still have it?

Billy   I have none of it. Didn't it all go on me medical bills at the time?

Bartley   You don't have even a quarter of it?

Billy   I don't. Why?

Bartley   No, only if you had a quarter of it you could probably buy yourself a pretty classy telescope, d'you know? Oh you could.

Helen   Do you have to bring telescopes into fecking everything, you?

Bartley   I don't, but I like to, ya bitch. Leave me!

Bartley *dashes out of the shop as* **Helen** *advances on him. Pause.*

Helen   I don't know where he gets the fecking cheek of him from, I don't.

Billy (*pause*)   How are ye two sailing to Inishmore, so, Helen? Ye've no boat.

Helen   We're getting Babbybobby Bennett to bring us in his boat.

Billy   Are you paying him?

Helen   Only in kisses and a bit of a hold of his hand, or I *hope* that it's only his hand I'll be holding. Although I've heard it's a big one. Jim Finnegan's daughter was telling me. She knows everybody's. I think she keeps a chart for herself.

Billy   She doesn't know mine.

Helen   And you say that like you're proud. I suppose she wasn't sure whether you had one, as mangled and fecked as you are.

Billy (*sadly*)   I have one.

Helen   Congratulations, but would you keep it to yourself? In more ways than one. (*Pause.*) Me, the only ones I've seen belong to priests. They keep showing them to me. I don't know why. I can't say they whetted me appetite. All brown. (*Pause.*) What have you gone all mopy for?

Billy   I don't know, now, but I suppose you intimating me mammy and daddy preferred death to being stuck with me didn't help matters.

Helen   I wasn't intimating that at all. I was saying it outright.

Billy (*quietly*)   You don't know what was in their heads.

Helen   Uh-huh? And do you?

Billy *bows his head sadly. Pause.* **Helen** *flicks him hard in the cheek with her finger, then moves off.*

Billy   Helen? Would Babbybobby be letting me go sailing to Inishmore with ye?

Helen   What have you to offer Babbybobby, sure? He wouldn't want to go holding *your* mangled hand.

Billy   What has Bartley to offer Bobby, so, and he's still going with ye?

Helen   Bartley said he'd help with the rowing. Could you help with the rowing?

Billy *lowers his head again.*

Helen   What would you want to be coming for, anyways?

Billy (*shrugging*)   To be in the filming.

Helen   You?

She starts laughing, slowly, moving to the door.

I shouldn't laugh at you, Billy . . . but I will.

She exits laughing. Pause. **Eileen** *returns from the back room and slaps* **Billy** *across the head.*

Billy   What was that fer?!

Eileen   Over my dead body are you going to Inishmore filming, Billy Claven!

Billy   Ah I was only thinking aloud, sure.

Eileen   Well stop thinking aloud! Stop thinking aloud and stop thinking quiet! There's too much oul thinking done in this house with you around. Did you ever see the Virgin Mary going thinking aloud?

Billy   I didn't.

Eileen   Is right, you didn't. And it didn't do her any harm!

Eileen *exits to the back room again. Pause.* **Billy** *gets up, shuffles to his mirror, looks himself over a moment, then sadly shuffles back to the table.* **Bartley** *opens the shop door and pops his head inside.*

Bartley   Cripple Billy, will you tell your aunty or your pretend aunty, I'll be in for me Mintios later, or, not me Mintios but me sweeties generally.

Billy   I will, Bartley.

Bartley   Me sister just told me your idea of being in the filming with us and I did have an awful laugh. That was a great joke, Billy.

Billy   Good-oh, Bartley.

Bartley   They may even bring you to Hollywood after. They may make a star out of ya.

Billy   They might at that, Bartley.

Bartley   A little cripple star. Heh. So you'll remind your aunty I'll be in for me Mintios later, or, not me Mintios but me . . .

Billy   Your sweeties generally.

Bartley   Me sweeties generally. Or if not later then tomorrow morning.

Billy   Goodbye, Bartley.

Bartley   Goodbye, Cripple Billy, or are you okay there, Cripple Billy, you do look a little bit sad for yourself?

Billy   I'm fine, Bartley.

Bartley   Good-oh.

Bartley *exits.* **Billy** *wheezes slightly, feeling his chest.*

Billy (*quietly*)   I'm fine, aye.

Pause. Blackout.

Scene Three

A shore at night. **Babbybobby** *fixing his curragh.* **Johnny** *enters, slightly drunk, walks up to him and watches a while.*

Johnny   I see you're getting your curragh ready, Babbybobby.

Bobby   I am, Johnnypateen.

Johnny (*pause*)   Are you getting your curragh ready so?

Bobby   Didn't I just say I was getting me curragh ready?

Johnny   You did, aye. (*Pause.*) So you're getting your curragh ready. (*Pause.*) All spick and span you're getting it. (*Pause.*) All nice and prepared like. (*Pause.*) All ready for a trip or something. (*Pause.*) That's a nice boat, that is. A nice boat for a tripeen. And it's even more nice now that you've got it all prepared for yourself. (*Pause.*) All prepared and ready.

Bobby   If it's a question you have to ask me, Johnnypateen, go ahead and ask me the question and don't be beating around the bush like some fool of an eejit schoolchild.

Johnny   I have no question to ask you. If Johnnypateen has a question to ask he comes right out and asks it. You don't see Johnnypateen beating around a bush. Oh no. (*Pause.*) Just commenting on how nice your curragh is is all. (*Pause.*) How nice and ready you're getting it. (*Pause.*) Nice and ready for a trip or something. (*Pause. Angrily.*) Well if you won't tell me where you're going I'll fecking be off with meself!

Bobby   Be off with yourself, aye.

Johnny   I *will* be off with meself. After your treatment!

Bobby   I gave you no treatment.

Johnny   You did give me treatment. You never tell me any news. Your Mrs up and died of TB the other year, and who was the last to know? *I* was the last to know. I wasn't told until the day she died, and you knew for weeks and weeks, with not a thought for my feelings . . .

Bobby I should've kicked her arse down the road to tell you, Johnnypateen, and, d'you know, I've regretted not doing so ever since.

Johnny One more time I'll say it so. So you're getting your curragh ready. All nice and prepared for a *trip* or something, now.

Bobby Ask me a question outright and I'll be pleased to give you the answer, Johnnypateen.

Johnny *stares at* **Bobby** *a second, fuming, then storms off.* **Bobby** *continues with the boat.*

Bobby (*quietly*) Ya stupid fecking eej. (*Pause. Calling off left.*) Who's that shuffling on the stones?

Billy (*off*) It's Billy Claven, Babbybobby.

Bobby I should've guessed that. Who else shuffles?

Billy (*entering*) No one, I suppose.

Bobby Are your aunties not worried you're out this late, Cripple Billy?

Billy They'd be worried if they knew but I snuck out on them.

Bobby You shouldn't sneak out on aunties, Cripple Billy. Even if they're funny aunties.

Billy Do you think they're funny aunties too, Babbybobby?

Bobby I saw your Aunty Kate talking to a stone one time.

Billy And she shouts at me for staring at cows.

Bobby Well I wouldn't hold staring at cows up as the height of sanity, Billy.

Billy Sure, I only stare at cows to get away from me aunties a while. It isn't for the fun of staring at cows. There *is* no fun in staring at cows. They just stand there looking at you like fools.

Bobby Do you never throw nothing at them cows? That might liven them up.

Billy I wouldn't want to hurt them, sure.

Bobby You're too kind-hearted is your trouble, Cripple Billy. Cows don't mind you throwing things at them. I threw a brick at a cow once and he didn't even moo, and I got him bang on the arse.

Billy Sure that's no evidence. He may've been a quiet cow.

Bobby He may've. And, sure, I'm not telling you to go pegging bricks at cows. I was drunk when this happened. Just if you get bored, I'm saying.

Billy I usually bring a book with me anyways. I've no desire to injure livestock.

Bobby You could throw the book at the cow.

Billy I would rather to read the book, Bobby.

Bobby It takes all kinds, as they say.

Billy It does. (*Pause.*) Are you getting your curragh ready there, Babbybobby?

Bobby Oh everybody's awful observant tonight, it does seem.

Billy Ready to bring Helen and Bartley o'er to the filming?

Bobby *looks at* **Billy** *a moment, checks out right to make sure* **Johnny** *isn't around, then returns.*

Bobby How did you hear tell of Helen and Bartley's travelling?

Billy Helen told me.

Bobby Helen told you. Jeez, and I told Helen she'd get a punch if she let anyone in on the news.

Billy I hear she's paying you in kisses for this boat-trip.

Bobby She is, and, sure, I didn't want paying at all. It was Helen insisted on that clause.

Billy   Wouldn't you want to kiss Helen, so?

Bobby   Ah, I get a bit scared of Helen, I do. She's awful fierce. (*Pause.*) Why, would you like to kiss Helen, Cripple Billy?

Billy *shrugs shyly, sadly.*

Billy   Ah I can't see Helen ever wanting to kiss a boy like me, anyways. Can you, Bobby?

Bobby   No.

Billy (*pause*)   But so you'd've took the McCormick's without payment at all?

Bobby   I would. I wouldn't mind having a look at this filming business meself. What harm in taking passengers along?

Billy   Would you take me as a passenger too, so?

Bobby (*pause*)   No.

Billy   Why, now?

Bobby   I've no room.

Billy   You've plenty of room.

Bobby   A cripple fella's bad luck in a boat, and everybody knows.

Billy   Since when, now?

Bobby   Since Poteen-Larry took a cripple fella in his boat and it sank.

Billy   That's the most ridiculous thing I've ever heard, Babbybobby.

Bobby   Or if he wasn't a cripple fella he had a bad leg on him anyways.

Billy   You're just prejudiced against cripples is all you are.

Bobby   I'm not at all prejudiced against cripples. I did kiss a cripple girl one time. Not only crippled but disfigured too. I was drunk, I didn't mind. You're not spoilt for pretty girls in Antrim.

Billy   Don't go changing the subject on me.

Bobby   Big green teeth. What subject?

Billy   The subject of taking me to the filming with ye.

Bobby   I thought we closed that subject.

Billy   We hardly opened that subject.

Bobby   Sure, what do you want to go to the filming for? They wouldn't want a cripple boy.

Billy   You don't know what they'd want.

Bobby   I don't, I suppose. No, you're right there. I did see a film there one time with a fella who not only had he no arms and no legs but he was a coloured fella too.

Billy   A coloured fella? I've never seen a coloured fella, let alone a crippled coloured fella. I didn't know you could get them.

Bobby   Oh they'd give you a terrible scare.

Billy   Coloured fellas? Are they fierce?

Bobby   They're less fierce with no arms or legs on them, because they can't do much to ya, but even so they're still fierce.

Billy   I heard a coloured fella a year ago came to Dublin a week.

Bobby   Ireland mustn't be such a bad place, so, if coloured fellas want to come to Ireland.

Billy   It mustn't. (*Pause.*) Ar, Babbybobby, you've only brought up coloured fellas to put me off the subject again.

Bobby   There's no cripple fellas coming in this boat, Billy. Maybe some day, in a year or two, like. If your feet straighten out on ya.

Billy   A year to two's no good to me, Bobby.

Bobby   Why so?

Billy *takes out a letter and hands it to* **Bobby**, *who starts reading it.*

Bobby   What's this?

Billy   It's a letter from Doctor McSharry, and you've got to promise you'll not breathe a word of it to another living soul.

Halfway through the letter, **Bobby**'s *expression saddens. He glances at* **Billy**, *then continues.*

Bobby   When did you get this?

Billy   Just a day ago I got it. (*Pause.*) Now will you let me come?

Bobby   Your aunties'll be upset at you going.

Billy   Well is it their life or is it my life? I'll send word to them from over there. Ah, I may only be gone a day or two anyways. I get bored awful easy. (*Pause.*) Will you let me come?

Bobby   Nine o'clock tomorrow morning be here.

Billy   Thank you, Bobby, I'll be here.

Bobby *gives him back the letter and* **Billy** *folds it away.* **Johnny** *quickly enters, his hand held out.*

Johnny   No, hang on there, now. What did the letter say?

Bobby   Ah Johnnypateen, will you feck off home for yourself?

Johnny   Be showing Johnnypateen that letter now, you, cripple-boy.

Billy   I won't be showing you me letter.

Johnny   What d'you mean you won't be showing me your letter? You showed *him* your letter. Be handing it over, now.

Billy   Did anybody ever tell you you're a biteen rude, Johnnypateenmike?

Johnny   *I'm* rude? *I'm* rude? With ye two standing there hogging letters, and letters from doctors is the most interesting kind of letters, and ye have the gall then to go calling *me* rude? Tell oul limpy to to be handing over that letter, now, else there'll be things I heard here tonight that won't stay secret much longer.

Bobby   Things like what, now?

Johnny   Oh, things like you rowing schoolies to Inishmore and you kissing green-teeth-girls in Antrim is the kind of thing, now. Not that I'm threatening blackmail on ya or anything, or, alright yes I am threatening blackmail on ya but a newsman has to obtain his news be hook or be crook.

Bobby   Be hook or be crook, is it? Well have this for hook or be crook.

Bobby *grabs* **Johnny** *by the hair and wrenches his arm up behind his back.*

Johnny   Aargh! Be letting go of me arm there you, ya thug! I'll get the constabulary on ya.

Bobby   Be lying down on the sand there, you, for yourself.

Bobby *forces* **Johnny** *face down on the ground.*

Johnny   Be running for the polis now you, cripple-boy, or shuffling anyways.

Billy   I won't. I'll be standing here watching.

Johnny   An accomplice that makes ya.

Billy   Good-oh.

Johnny   I'm only an oul fella.

Bobby *steps up onto* **Johnny**'s *backside.*

Johnny   Aargh! Get off of me arse, you!

Bobby   Billy, go pick up somes stones for me.

Billy (*doing so*)   Big stones?

Bobby   Middling-size stones.

Johnny   What do you want stones for?

Bobby   To peg them at your head 'til you promise not to bandy me business about town.

Johnny   You'll never get me to make such a promise. I can withstand any torture. Like Kevin Barry I am.

Bobby *throws a stone at* **Johnny***'s head.*

Johnny   Aargh! I promise, I promise.

Bobby   On Christ ya promise?

Johnny   On Christ I promise.

Bobby   That withstanding didn't last fecking long.

Bobby *gets off* **Johnny***, who stands back up, brushing himself off.*

Johnny   I wouldn't get that kind of treatment in England! And now I have sand in me ears.

Bobby   Take that sand home with ya and show it to your drunken mammy so.

Johnny   You leave my drunken mammy out of it.

Bobby   And be remembering that promise.

Johnny   Under duress that promise was made.

Bobby   I don't care if it was made under a dog's arsehole. You'll be remembering it.

Johnny (*pause*)   Ya feckers, ya!

Johnny *storms off right, shaking his fist.*

Bobby   I've wanted to peg stones at that man's head for fifteen years.

Billy   I'd never get up the courage to peg stones at his head.

Bobby   Ah, I suppose you shouldn't peg stones at an oul fella's head, but didn't he drive me to it? (*Pause.*) You got up the courage to travel to Inishmore anyways, and you scared of the sea.

Billy   I did. (*Pause.*) We'll meet at nine tomorrow so.

Bobby   Better make it eight, Cripple Billy, in case Johnnypateen lets the cat out of the bag.

Billy   Do you not trust him so?

Bobby   I'd trust him as much as I'd trust you to carry a pint for me without spilling it.

Billy   That's not a nice thing to say.

Bobby   I'm a hard character, me.

Billy   You're not a hard character at all, Babbybobby. You're a soft character.

Bobby (*pause*)   My wife Annie died of the same thing, d'you know? TB. But at least I got a year to spend with her. Three months is no time.

Billy   I won't even see the summer in. (*Pause.*) D'you remember the time Annie made me the jam roly-poly when I had the chicken-pox? And the smile she gave me then?

Bobby   Was it a nice jam roly-poly?

Billy (*reluctantly*)   Not really, Bobby.

Bobby   No. Poor Annie couldn't cook jam roly-polies to save the life of her. Ah, I still miss her, despite her awful puddings. (*Pause.*) I'm glad I was able to help you in some way anyways, Cripple Billy, in the time you've left.

Billy   Would you do me a favour, Babbybobby? Would you not call me Cripple Billy any more long?

Bobby   What do you want to be called so?

Billy   Well, just Billy.

Bobby   Oh. Okay so, Billy.

Billy   And you, would you rather just be called Bobby and not Babbybobby?

Bobby   For why?

Billy   I don't know why.

Bobby   I do like being called Babbybobby. What's wrong with it?

Billy   Nothing at all, I suppose. I'll see you in the morning so, Babbybobby.

Bobby   See you in the morning so, Cripple Billy. Em, *Billy*.

Billy   Didn't I just say?

Bobby   I forgot. I'm sorry, Billy.

Billy *nods, then shuffles away.*

Bobby   Oh, and Billy?

Billy *looks back.* **Bobby** *makes a gesture with his hand.*

Bobby   I'm sorry.

Billy *bows his head, nods, and exits right. Pause.* **Bobby** *notices something in the surf, picks a bible up out of it, looks at it a moment, then tosses it back into the sea and continues working on the boat. Blackout.*

Scene Four

Bedroom of **Mammy O'Dougal**, **Johnny**'s *ninety-year-old mother.* **Mammy** *in bed,* **Doctor McSharry** *checking her with a stethoscope,* **Johnny** *hovering.*

Doctor   Have you been laying off the drink, Mrs O'Dougal?

Johnny   Did you not hear me question, Doctor?

Doctor   I did hear your question, but amn't I trying to examine your mammy without your fool questions?

Johnny   Fool questions, is it?

Doctor   Have you been laying off the drink, Mrs O'Dougal, I said?

Mammy (*burps*)   I *have* been laying off the drink or I've sort of been laying off the drink.

Johnny   She has a pint of porter now and then is no harm at all.

Mammy   Is no harm at all.

Johnny   Is good for you!

Doctor   So long as you keep it at a pint of porter is the main thing so.

Mammy   It *is* the main thing, and a couple of whiskies now and then.

Johnny   Didn't I only just say not to mention the whiskies, ya thick?

Doctor   How often is now and then?

Johnny   Once in a blue moon.

Mammy   Once in a blue moon, and at breakfast sometimes.

Johnny   'At breakfast', jeez . . .

Doctor   Johnnypateenmike, don't you know well not to go feeding a ninety-year-old woman whiskey for breakfast?

Johnny   Ah she likes it, and doesn't it shut her up?

Mammy   I do like a drop of whiskey, me, I do.

Johnny   From the horse's mouth.

Mammy   Although I do prefer poteen.

Doctor   But you don't get given poteen?

Mammy   I don't get given poteen, no.

Johnny   *Now.*

Mammy   Only on special occasions.

Doctor   And what qualifies as a special occasion?

Mammy   A Friday, a Saturday or a Sunday.

Doctor   When your mammy's dead and gone, Johnnypateen, I'm going to cut out her liver and show it to you, the damage your fine care has done.

Johnny   You won't catch me looking at me mammy's liver. I can barely stomach the outside of her, let alone the inside.

Doctor   A fine thing that is for a fella to say in front of his mammy.

Mammy   I've heard worse.

Johnny   Leave me mammy alone now, you, with your mangling. If she's been trying to drink herself dead for sixty-five years with no luck, I wouldn't start worrying about her now. Sixty-five years. Feck, she can't do anything right.

Doctor   Why do you want to drink yourself dead, Mrs O'Dougal?

Mammy   I do miss me husband Donal. Ate be a shark.

Johnny   1871 he was ate be a shark.

Doctor   Oh you should be trying to get over that now, Mrs O'Dougal.

Mammy   I've tried to, Doctor, but I can't. A lovely man he was. And living with this goose all these years, it just brings it back to me.

Johnny   Who are you calling a goose, ya hairy-lipped fool? Didn't I go out of me way to bring Doctor McSharry home to ya?

Mammy   Aye, but only to go nosing about Cripple Billy Claven is all.

Johnny   No, not . . . not . . . Ah you always go spilling the beans, you, ya lump.

Mammy   I'm an honest woman, me, Johnnypateen.

Johnny   Honest me hairy hole.

Mammy   And you didn't get me drunk enough.

The **Doctor** *packs up his black bag.*

Doctor   If I'm only here under false pretences . . .

Johnny   You're not here under false pretences. Me mammy did seem awful bad earlier . . . cough, Mammy . . .

Mammy *coughs*.

Johnny But she seems to be over the worst of it, you're right there, although, now, while you're here, Doctor, what *is* all this about Cripple Billy? He wouldn't be in a terrible way, would he? Maybe something life-threatening, now? Oh I suppose it must be something awful serious if you go writing letters to him.

Doctor (*pause*) Did you ever hear of a thing called doctor-patient confidentiality, Johnnypateenmike?

Johnny I did, and I think it's a great thing. Now tell me what's wrong with Cripple Billy, Doctor.

Doctor I'm going to open up that head of yours one day, Johnnypateen, and find nothing inside it at all.

Johnny Don't go straying off the subject now, you. Tell me what's wrong with . . . or was that a clue to the subject, now? There's something on the inside of his head that's wrong? A brain tumour? He has a brain tumour!

Doctor I wasn't aware . . .

Johnny Tell me he has a brain tumour, Doctor. Oh that'd be awful big news.

Doctor I'm off home, I thank you for wasting me precious time, but before I go I'll just say one thing, and that's I don't know where you got your information from this time o'er Cripple Billy, for it's usually such accurate information you do get, oh aye . . .

Johnny Polio, polio. He has polio.

Doctor But as far as I'm aware, apart from those deformities he's had since birth, there is nothing wrong with Billy Claven at all, and it would be better if you didn't go spreading fool gossip about him.

Johnny (*pause*) TB. TB. Ah it must be TB.

The **Doctor** *walks away*.

Johnny Where are you off to? Don't go hogging all the decent news, you!

The **Doctor** *has exited*.

Johnny   Ya beggar! Is Billy in such good health that rowing to Inishmore in the freezing morning as he did this day'll do him no harm, so?

Pause. The **Doctor** *returns, thoughtful*.

Johnny   Didn't that get him running back quick?

Mammy   Like a cat with a worm up his arse.

Doctor   Billy's gone to Inishmore?

Johnny   He has. With the McCormicks and Babbybobby rowing them. Babbybobby who'll be arrested for grievous bodily harm the minute he returns, or grievous *headily* harm anyways, for it was me head he grievously harmed.

Doctor   They've gone to see the filming?

Johnny   To see the filming or to be in the filming, aye.

Doctor   But the filming finished yesterday, sure. It's only clearing the oul cameras and whatnot they are today.

Johnny (*pause*)   I suppose they must've been given unreliable information somewhere along the way, so.

Mammy   Aye, be this goose.

Johnny   Don't you be calling me goose, I said.

Mammy   Get me a drink, goose.

Johnny   If you retract goose I'll get you a dr . . .

Mammy   I retract goose.

Johnny *pours her a large whiskey, the* **Doctor** *aghast*.

Doctor   Don't . . . don't . . . (*Angrily*.) Have I been talking to meself all day?!

Johnny (*pause*)   Would you like a drink too, Doctor, after I have stunned you with me Cripple Billy revelation?

Doctor   What do I care about that arse-faced revelation?

Johnny   Heh. We'll see if your tune's the same when Billy returns home dead because of your secrecy, and you're drummed out of doctorhood and forced to scrape the skitter out of bent cows, is all you were ever really fit for anyways, oh we all know.

Doctor   Billy won't be returning home dead because there's nothing the matter with Billy but a wheeze.

Johnny   Are you persisting in that one, Doctor Useless?

Doctor   Shall I say it one more time, thicko? There is nothing wrong with Billy Claven. Okay?

The **Doctor** *exits.*

Johnny   Cancer! Cancer! Come back you! Would it be cancer? Tell me what it begins with. Is it a 'C'? Is it a 'P'?

Mammy   You're talking to thin air, ya fool.

Johnny (*calling*)   I'll get to the bottom of it one way or the other, McSharry! Be hook or be crook! A good newsman never takes no for an answer!

Mammy   No. You just take stones pegged at your head for an answer.

Johnny   Let the stone matter drop, I've told you twenty times, or I'll kick your black arse back to Antrim for you.

Johnny *sits on the bed, reading a newspaper.*

Mammy   You and your shitey-arsed news.

Johnny   My news isn't shitey-arsed. My news is great news. Did you hear Jack Ellery's goose and Pat Brennan's cat have both been missing a week? I suspect something awful's happened to them, or I *hope* something awful's happened to them.

Mammy   Even though you're me own son I'll say it, Johnnypateen, you're the most boring oul fecker in Ireland. And there's plenty of competition for that fecking post!

Johnny   There's a sheep here in Kerry with no ears, I'll have to make a note.

Mammy (*pause*)   Give me the bottle if you're going bringing up sheep deformities.

He gives her the whiskey bottle.

Johnny   Sheep deformities is interesting news. Is the best kind of news. Excluding major illnesses anyways. (*Pause.*) And I want to see half that bottle gone be tea-time.

Mammy   Poor Cripple Billy. The life that child's had. With that mam and dad of his, and that sackful of stones of theirs . . .

Johnny   Shut up about the sackful of stones.

Mammy   And now this. Although look at the life I've had too. First poor Donal bit in two, then you going thieving the hundred-pound floorboard money he'd worked all his life to save and only to piss it away in pubs. Then the beetroot fecking paella you go making every Tuesday on top of it.

Johnny   There's nothing the matter with beetroot paella, and hasn't half of that hundred pounds been poured down your dribbling gob the past sixty years, ya bollocks?

Mammy   Poor Billy. It's too many of the coffins of gosawers I've seen laid in the ground in me time.

Johnny   Drink up, so. You may save yourself the trouble this time.

Mammy   Ah, I'm holding out to see you in your coffin first, Johnnypat. Wouldn't that be a happy day?

Johnny   Isn't that funny, because I'd enjoy seeing *you* in *your* coffin the same as ya, if we can find a coffin big enough to squeeze your fat arse into. Course we may have to saw half the blubber off you first, oh there's not even a question.

Mammy   Oh you've upset me awful with them harsh remarks, Johnnypateen, oh aye. (*Pause.*) Ya fecking eejit. (*Pause.*) Anything decent in the paper, read it out to me. But no sheep news.

Johnny   There's a fella here, riz to power in Germany, has an awful funny moustache on him.

Mammy   Let me see his funny moustache.

He shows her the photo.

That's a funny moustache.

Johnny   You'd think he'd either grow a proper moustache or else shave that poor biteen of a straggle off.

Mammy   That fella seems to be caught in two minds.

Johnny   Ah he seems a nice enough fella, despite his funny moustache. Good luck to him. (*Pause.*) There's a German fella living out in Connemara now, d'you know? Out Leenane way.

Mammy   Ireland mustn't be such a bad place if German fellas want to come to Ireland.

Johnny   They all want to come to Ireland, sure. Germans, dentists, everybody.

Mammy   And why, I wonder?

Johnny   Because in Ireland the people are more friendly.

Mammy   They are, I suppose.

Johnny   Of course they are, sure. Everyone knows that. Sure, isn't it what we're famed for? (*Long pause.*) I'd bet money on cancer.

Johnny *nods, returning to his paper. Blackout.*

Scene Five

The shop. A few dozen eggs stacked on counter.

Kate   Not a word. (*Pause.*) Not a word, not a word, not a word, not a word, not a word, not a word, not a word. (*Pause.*) Not a word.

Eileen   Oh how many more times are you going to say 'Not a word', Kate?

Kate   Am I not allowed to say 'Not a word' so, and me terrified o'er Billy's travellings?

Eileen   You *are* allowed to say 'Not a word', but one or two times and not ten times.

Kate   Billy's going to go the same way as his mammy and daddy went. Dead and buried be the age of twenty.

Eileen   Do you ever look on the optimistic side, you?

Kate   I do look on the optimistic side, but I fear I'll never see poor Billy alive again.

Eileen (*pause*)   Billy could've at least left a note that he was going to Inishmore, and not have us hear it from oul Johnnypateen.

Kate   Not a word. Not a word, not a word, not a word.

Eileen   And Johnnypateen revelling in his news-telling then, along with his intimating o'er letters and doctors.

Kate   I fear Johnnypateen knows something about Billy he's not telling.

Eileen   When has Johnnypateen ever known something and not told, sure? Johnnypateen tells if a horse farts.

Kate   Do you think?

Eileen   I know.

Kate   I still worry o'er Cripple Billy.

Eileen   Sure, if McSharry's right that the filming's o'er, it won't be long at all before Billy's home, and the rest of them with him.

Kate   You said that last week and they're still not home.

Eileen   Maybe they stayed to see the sights.

Kate   On Inishmore? What sights? A fence and a hen?

Eileen   Maybe a cow came o'er to Cripple Billy and he lost track of time.

Kate   It doesn't take much time to look at a cow, sure.

Eileen   Well, you used to take an age in talking to stones, I remember.

Kate Them stone days were when I had trouble with me nerves and you know well they were, Eileen! Didn't we agree on never bringing the stones business up!

Eileen We did, and I'm sorry for bringing the stones business up. It's only because I'm as worried as ya that I let them stones slip.

Kate Because people who live in glass houses shouldn't throw stone-conversations at me.

Eileen What glass house do I live in?

Kate We had twenty Yalla-mallows in the ha'penny box the other day and I see they're all gone. How are we ever to make a profit if you keep eating the new sweeties before anybody's had a chance to see them?

Eileen Ah, Kate. Sure with Yalla-mallows, when you eat one, there's no stopping ya.

Kate It was the same excuse with the Mintios. Well if you lay one finger on the Fripple-Frapples when they come in, you'll be for the high jump, I'm telling ya.

Eileen I'm sorry, Kate. It's just all this worry o'er Billy didn't help matters.

Kate I know it didn't, Eileen. I know you like to stuff your face when you're worried. Just try to keep a lid on it is all.

Eileen I will. (*Pause.*) Ah sure that Babbybobby's a decent enough fella. He'll be looking after Billy, I'm sure.

Kate Why did he bring poor Billy off with him anyways so if he's such a decent fella? Didn't he know his aunties would be worrying?

Eileen I don't know if he knew.

Kate I'd like to hit Babbybobby in the teeth.

Eileen I suppose he . . .

Kate With a brick.

Eileen I suppose he could've got Billy to send a note at the minimum.

Kate   Not a word. Not a word. (*Pause.*) Not a word, not a word, not a wor . . .

Eileen   Ah, Kate, don't be starting with your 'Not a words' again.

Kate *watches* **Eileen** *stacking the eggs a while.*

Kate   I see the egg-man's been.

Eileen   He has. The egg-man has a rake more eggs when Slippy Helen doesn't be working for him.

Kate   I don't see why he keeps Helen on at all.

Eileen   I think he's afraid of Helen. That or he's in love with Helen.

Kate (*pause*)   I think Billy's in love with Helen on top of it.

Eileen   *I* think Billy's in love with Helen. It'll all end in tears.

Kate   Tears or death.

Eileen   We ought look on the bright side.

Kate   Tears, death or worse.

Johnny *enters, strutting.*

Eileen   Johnnypateenmike.

Kate   Johnnypateenmike.

Johnny   Johnnypateen does have three pieces of news to be telling ye this day.

Kate   Only tell us if it's happy news, Johnnypat, because we're a biteen depressed today, we are.

Johnny   I have a piece of news concerning the Inishmore trippers, but I will be saving that piece of news for me third piece of news.

Kate   Is Billy okay, Johnnypateen? Oh tell us that piece of news first.

Eileen   Tell us that piece of news first, aye, Johnnypateen.

Johnny   Well if ye're going arranging what order I tell me pieces of news in, I think I will turn on me heels and be off with me!

Kate   Don't go, Johnnypat! Don't go!

Johnny   Hah?

Eileen   Tell us your news in whatever order you like, Johnnypateen. Sure, aren't you the man who knows best about news-ordering?

Johnny   I *am* the man who knows best. I *know* I'm the man who knows best. That's no news. I see you have plenty of eggs in.

Eileen   We do, Johnnypateen.

Johnny   Uh-huh. Me first piece of news, there is a sheep out in Kerry with no ears at all on him.

Eileen (*pause*)   That's a great piece of news.

Johnny   Don't ask me how he hears because I don't know and I don't care. Me second piece of news, Patty Brennan's cat was found dead and Jack Ellery's goose was found dead and nobody in town is said to've seen anything, but we can all put two and two together, although not out loud because Jack Ellery's an awful tough.

Kate   That's a sad piece of news because now it sounds like a feud is starting.

Johnny   A feud is starting and won't be stopped 'til the one or the two of them finish up slaughtered. Good. I will take six eggs, Mrs, for the omelette I promised me mammy a fortnight ago.

Eileen   What was the third piece of news, Johnnypateen?

Johnny   I mention me mammy and nobody even asks as to how she is. Oh it's the height of politeness in this quarter.

Kate   How is your mammy, Johnnypateen?

Johnny   Me mammy's fine, so she is, despite me best efforts.

Eileen   Are you still trying to kill your mammy with the drink, Johnnypateen?

Johnny   I am but it's no use. A fortune in booze that bitch has cost me over the years. She'll never go. (*Pause.*) Well now, I have me eggs, I've told you me two pieces of news. I suppose that's me business finished here for the day.

Kate   The . . . the third piece of news, Johnnypateen?

Johnny   Oh, the third piece of news. Wasn't I almost forgetting? (*Pause.*) The third piece of news is Babbybobby's just pulled his boat up on the sands, at the headland there, and let the young adventurers off. Or, let *two* of the young adventurers off anyways, Helen and Bartley. There was no hide nor hair of Cripple Billy in that boat. (*Pause.*) I'm off to have Babbybobby arrested for throwing stones at me head. I thank you for the eggs.

Johnny *exits. Pause.* **Kate** *sadly caresses the old sack hanging on the wall, then sits at the table.*

Kate   He's gone from us, Eileen. He's gone from us.

Eileen   We don't know at all that he's gone from us.

Kate   I can feel it in me bones, Eileen. From the minute he left I knew. Cripple Billy's dead and gone.

Eileen   But didn't the doctor assure us five times there was nothing wrong with Cripple Billy?

Kate   Only so not to hurt us that assuring was. It was Johnnypat who had the real story all along, same as about Billy's mam and dad's drowning he always had the real story.

Eileen   Oh lord, I see Babbybobby coming up the pathway towards us.

Kate   Does he look glum, Eileen?

Eileen   He does look glum, but Babbybobby usually looks glum.

Kate   Does he look glummer than he usually looks?

Eileen (*pause*)   He does.

Kate Oh no.

Eileen And he's taken the hat off him now.

Kate That's an awful bad sign, taking the hat off ya.

Eileen Maybe just being gentlemanly he is?

Kate Babbybobby? Sure, Babbybobby pegs bricks at cows.

Bobby *enters, cap in hand.*

Bobby Eileen, Kate.

Eileen Babbybobby.

Bobby Would you be sitting down a minute there for yourself, now, Eileen? I've news to be telling ye.

Eileen *sits at the table.*

Bobby I've just brought the two McCormicks home, and I was supposed to bring yere Billy home, I know, but I couldn't bring yere Billy home because . . . because he's been taken to America for a screen test for a film they're making about a cripple fella. Or . . . I don't think the *whole* film will be about the cripple fella. The cripple fella'd only be a minor role. Aye. But it'd still be a good part, d'you know? (*Pause.*) Although, there's more important things in the world than good parts in Hollywood films about cripple fellas. Being around your family and your friends is more important, and I tried to tell Cripple Billy that, but he wouldn't listen to me, no matter how much I told him. Be boat this morning they left. Billy wrote a letter here he asked me to pass onto ye. (*Pause.*) Two or three months at minimum, Billy said probably he'd be gone. (*Pause.*) Ah, as he said to me, it's his life. I suppose it is, now. I hope he enjoys his time there anyways. (*Pause.*) That's all there is. (*Pause.*) I'll be seeing ye.

Eileen Be seeing you, Babbybobby . . .

Kate Be seeing you, Bobbybabbybobby.

Bobby *exits.* **Kate** *opens the letter.*

Eileen What the devil's a screen test, Kate?

Kate   I don't know at all what a screen test is.

Eileen   Maybe in his letter it says.

Kate   Oh the awful handwriting he has.

Eileen   It's never improved.

Kate   'Dear Aunties, can ye guess what?' Yes, we *can* guess what. 'I am off to Hollywood to make a screen test for a film they're making, and if they like the look of me a contract they will give me and an actor then I'll be.' He doesn't explain at all what a screen test is.

Eileen   With all the thinking he does?

Kate   What's this now? I can't make out even two words in this sentence with his writing . . . 'But if it's a big success I am . . . it might only be two or three months before I am too busy with acting work to be getting in touch with ye too often at all . . . so if ye don't hear from me much from summertime on . . . don't be worrying about me. It'll only mean I'm happy and healthy and making a go of me life in America. Making something of meself for ye and mammy and daddy to be proud of. Give my love to everyone on the island except Johnnypateen, and take care of yourselves, Kate and Eileen. You moan the world to me . . . *mean* the world to me.' It looks like 'moan'. (*Pause.*) 'Yours sincerely . . . Billy Claven.' (*Pause.*) Turned his back on us, he has, Eileen.

Eileen (*crying*)   And us worrying our heads off o'er him.

Eileen *goes to the counter and quietly fishes through the sweetie box.*

Kate   After all we've done for him down the years.

Eileen   We looked after him and didn't care that he was a cripple-boy at all.

Kate   After all the shame he brought on us, staring at cows, and this is how he repays us.

Eileen   I hope the boat sinks before it ever gets him to America.

Kate I hope he drowns like his mammy and daddy drowned before him.

Eileen (*pause*)   Or are we being too harsh on him?

Kate (*crying*)   We're being too harsh on him but only because it's so upset about him we are. What are you eating?

Eileen Oh Yalla-mallows and don't be starting on me.

Kate I thought you'd ate all the Yalla-mallows.

Eileen I'd put a couple of Yalla-mallows aside for emergencies.

Kate Eat ahead, Eileen.

Eileen Do you want one, Kate?

Kate I don't. I have no stomach for eating at all, this day. Let alone eating Yalla-mallows.

Eileen (*pause*)   We'll see Cripple Billy again one day, won't we, Kate?

Kate I fear we've more chance of seeing Jim Finnegan's daughter in a nunnery before we see Cripple Billy again. (*Pause.*) I'm not sure if I *want* to see Cripple Billy again.

Eileen I'm not sure if *I* want to see Cripple Billy again. (*Pause.*) I want to see Cripple Billy again.

Kate *I* want to see Cripple Billy again.

Pause. Blackout.

Interval.

Scene Six

The shop, summer, four months later. A couple of flyers for Man of Aran, *being shown at the church hall, hang on the walls. The sweetie boxes and a stone lie on the counter, beside which* **Bartley** *stands, pursing his lips dumbly and doing other stuff for a few moments to fill in time as he waits for* **Kate** *to return.* **Helen** *enters carrying a few dozen eggs.*

Helen What are you waiting for?

Bartley   She's gone in the back to look for me Fripple-Frapples.

Helen   Oh you and your fecking Fripple-Frapples.

Bartley   Fripple-Frapples are nice sweeties.

Helen *arranges the eggs on the counter*.

Barley   I see you've brought the eggs up.

Helen   You, you're awful observant.

Bartley   I thought bringing the eggs was the egg-man's job.

Helen   It *was* the egg-man's job, but I did kick the egg-man in the shins this after and he didn't feel up to it.

Bartley   What did you kick the egg-man in the shins for?

Helen   He insinuated it was me murdered Jack Ellery's goose and Pat Brennan's cat for them.

Bartley   But it *was* you murdered Jack Ellery's goose and Pat Brennan's cat for them.

Helen   I know it was, but if it gets bandied around town I'll never be getting paid.

Bartley   How much are you getting paid?

Helen   Eight bob for the goose and ten bob for the cat.

Bartley   Why did you charge extra for the cat?

Helen   Well, I had to pay Ray Darcy for the borrow of his axe. See, the goose I only had to stomp on him. It takes more than a stomp to polish a cat off.

Bartley   A plankeen of wood you could've used on the cat, and saved shelling out for the axe at all.

Helen   Sure I wanted the job carried out professional, Bartley. A plank is the weapon of a flat-faced child. I wouldn't use a plank on a blue-arsed fly.

Bartley   What *would* you use on a blue-arsed fly?

Helen I wouldn't use a thing on a blue-arsed fly. There's no money involved in killing blue-arsed flies.

Bartley Jim Finnegan's daughter killed twelve worms one day.

Helen Aye, be breathing on them.

Bartley No, be sticking needles in their eyes.

Helen Now there's the work of an amateur. (*Pause.*) I didn't even know worms had eyes.

Bartley They don't after Jim Finnegan's daughter gets through with them.

Helen What's this stone here for?

Bartley I caught Mrs Osbourne talking to that stone when first I came in.

Helen What was she saying to the stone?

Bartley She was saying 'How are you, stone', and then putting the stone to her ear like the stone was talking back to her.

Helen That's awful strange behaviour.

Bartley And asking the stone, then, if it knew how oul Cripple Billy was doing for himself in America.

Helen And what did the stone say?

Bartley (*pause*) The stone didn't say anything, Helen, because stones they don't say anything.

Helen Oh, I thought you said Mrs Osbourne was doing the voice for the stone.

Bartley No, Mrs Osbourne was just doing her own voice.

Helen Maybe we should hide the stone and see if Mrs Osbourne has a nervous breakdown.

Bartley Sure that wouldn't be a very Christian thing to do, Helen.

Helen   It wouldn't be a very Christian thing to do, no, but it'd be awful funny.

Bartley   Ah let's leave Mrs Osbourne's stone alone, Helen. Hasn't she enough on her mind worrying o'er Cripple Billy?

Helen   Cripple Billy's aunties should be *told* that Billy's dead or dying, and not have them waiting for a letter from him that'll never come. Four months, now, isn't it they've been waiting, and not a word, and them the only two on Inishmaan not been informed what Babbybobby knows.

Bartley   What good would it do, sure, informing them? At least this way they've the hope he's still alive. What help would Babbybobby's news be to them? And you never know but maybe a miracle's happened and Cripple Billy hasn't died in Hollywood at all. Maybe three months wasn't a fair estimate for Cripple Billy.

Helen   I hope Cripple Billy *has* died in Hollywood, after taking his place in Hollywood that was rightfully a pretty girl's place, when he knew full well he was about to kick the bucket.

Bartley   A pretty girl's place? What use would a pretty girl be in playing a cripple fella?

Helen   I could turn me hand to anything, me, given a chance.

Bartley   I've heard.

Helen   Heard what?

Bartley   I've heard Hollywood is chock-full of pretty girls, sure. It's cripple fellas they're crying out for.

Helen   What are you defending Cripple Billy for? Didn't he promise to send you a package of Yalla-mallows you've never seen a lick of?

Bartley   Maybe Cripple Billy died before he had a chance of sending me them Yalla-mallows.

Helen   It's any excuse for you, ya weed.

Bartley   But dying's an awful good excuse for not sending a fella the sweeties he promised.

Helen   Too kind-hearted you are. I'm ashamed to admit you're related to me sometimes.

Bartley   It doesn't hurt to be too kind-hearted.

Helen   Uh-huh. Does this hurt?

Helen *pinches* **Bartley**'*s arm.*

Bartley (*in pain*)   No.

Helen (*pause*)   Does this hurt?

Helen *gives him a Chinese burn on the forearm.*

Bartley (*in pain*)   No.

Helen (*pause*)   Does this hurt?

Helen *picks up an egg and breaks it against his forehead.*

Bartley (*sighing*)   I'd better say yes before any further you go.

Helen   You should've said yes on the arm pinch, would've been using your brain.

Bartley   I should've said yes but you'd still've broken an egg on me.

Helen   Now we'll never know.

Bartley   You're just a terror when you get around eggs.

Helen   I do like breaking eggs on fellas.

Bartley   I had guessed that somehow.

Helen   Or could you classify you as a fella? Isn't that going a biteen overboard?

Bartley   I notice you never broke an egg on Babbybobby Bennett when he reneged on your kissing proposals.

Helen   We were in a row-boat a mile from land, sure. Where was I supposed to get an egg?

Bartley   Reneged because you're so witchy-looking.

Helen   Reneged because he was upset o'er Cripple Billy, and watch your 'witchy-looking' comments, you.

Bartley   Why is it runny eggs don't smell but boiled eggs do smell?

Helen   I don't know why. And I don't care why.

Bartley   Reneged because you look like one of them ragged-looking widow women waiting on the rocks for a rascal who'll never return to her.

Helen   That sentence had an awful lot of Rs.

Bartley   It was insulting with it, on top of the Rs.

Helen   You've gotten awful cocky for a boy with egg running down his gob.

Bartley   Well there comes a time for every Irishman to take a stand against his oppressors.

Helen   Was it Michael Collins said that?

Bartley   It was some one of the fat ones anyways.

Helen   Do you want to play 'England versus Ireland'?

Bartley   I don't know how to play 'England versus Ireland'.

Helen   Stand here and close your eyes. You'll be Ireland.

Bartley *faces her and closes his eyes.*

Bartley   And what do you do?

Helen   I'll be England.

Helen *picks up three eggs from the counter and breaks the first against* **Bartley**'*s forehead.* **Bartley** *opens his eyes as the yolk runs down him, and stares at her sadly.* **Helen** *breaks the second egg on his forehead.*

Bartley   That wasn't a nice thing at all to . . .

Helen   Haven't finished.

Helen *breaks the third egg on* **Bartley**.

Bartley   That wasn't a nice thing at all to do, Helen.

Helen   I was giving you a lesson about Irish history,
Bartley.

Bartley   I don't need a lesson about Irish history.
(*Shouting*.) Or anyways not with eggs when I've only washed
me hair!

Helen   There'll be worse casualties than eggy hair before
Ireland's a nation once again, Bartley McCormick.

Bartley   And me best jumper, look at it!

Helen   It has egg on it.

Bartley   I know it has egg on it! I know well! And I was
going to go wearing it to the showing of the film tomorrow,
but you've put paid to that idea now, haven't ya?

Helen   I'm looking forward to the showing of the film
tomorrow.

Bartley   I was looking forward to the showing of the film
too until me jumper became destroyed.

Helen   I think I might go pegging eggs at the film
tomorrow. The *Man of Aran* me arsehole. 'The Lass of Aran'
they could've had, and the *pretty* lass of Aran. Not some oul
shite about thick fellas fecking fishing.

Bartley   Does everything you do have to involve egg-
pegging, Helen?

Helen   I do take a pride in me egg-work, me. Is this bitch
never bloody coming to pay for me eggs? (*Calling*.) You,
stonewoman!

Bartley   She's taking an age to bring me Fripple-Frapples.

Helen   Ah I can't waste me youth waiting for that mingy
hole. You collect me egg-money, Bartley, and give it to the
egg-man on the way home.

Bartley   I will, Helen, aye.

Helen *exits*.

Bartley   I will me fecking arse, ya shite-gobbed fecking
bitch-fecker, ya . . .

Helen *pops her head back in.*

Helen   And don't let her dock you for the four you went and broke on me.

Bartley   I won't, Helen.

She exits again.

(*Sighing.*) Women.

Kate *slowly enters from the back room, absent-mindedly, noticing* **Bartley** *after a second.*

Kate   Hello there, Bartley. What can I be getting for ya?

Bartley (*pause. Bemused*)   You were going in the back to look for your Fripple-Frapples, Mrs.

Kate *thinks to herself a moment, then slowly returns to the back room.* **Bartley** *moans loudly in frustration, putting his head down on the counter. Slight pause, then* **Kate** *returns and picks up her stone.*

Kate   I'll bring me stone.

She exits to the back room again. Pause. **Bartley** *picks up a wooden mallet, smashes all the eggs on the counter with it and walks out, slamming the door. Blackout.*

Scene Seven

Sound of **Billy**'s *wheezing starts, as lights come up on him shivering alone on a chair in a squalid Hollywood hotel room. He wheezes slightly throughout.*

Billy   Mam? I fear I'm not longer for this world, Mam. Can't I hear the wail of the banshees for me, as far as I am from me barren island home? A home barren, aye, but proud and generous with it, yet turned me back on ye I did, to end up alone and dying in a one-dollar rooming-house, without a mother to wipe the cold sweat off me, nor a father to curse God o'er the death of me, nor a colleen fair to weep tears o'er the still body of me. A body still, aye, but a body noble and unbowed with it. An Irishman! (*Pause.*) *Just* an Irishman. With a decent heart on him, and a decent head on him, and a

decent spirit not broken by a century's hunger and a
lifetime's oppression! A spirit not broken, no . . . (*Coughing*.)
but a body broken, and the lungs of him broken, and, if truth
be told, the heart of him broken too, be a lass who never knew
his true feelings, and now, sure, never will. What's this,
Mammy, now, that you're saying to me?

He looks at a sheet of paper on the table.

Be writing home to her, I know, and make me feelings
known. Ah, tis late, Mammy. Won't tomorrow be soon
enough for that task?

*He gets up and shuffles to the mirror left, quietly singing 'The Croppy
Boy'.*

'Farewell Father and Mother too, and sister Mary I have
none but you. And for my brother, he's all alone. He's
pointing pikes on the grinding stone.'

*He stumbles, ill, crawls up onto the bed, wheezing, and looks at the
photo on the dresser.*

What would Heaven be like, Mammy? I've heard 'tis a
beautiful place, more beautiful than Ireland even, but even if
it is, sure, it wouldn't be near as beautiful as you. I do wonder
would they let cripple boys into Heaven at all. Sure,
wouldn't we only go uglifying the place?

He puts the photo back on the dresser.

'Twas in old Ireland this young man died, and in old Ireland
his body's lain. All the good people that do pass by, may the
lord have mercy on this croppy boy.' Oh it's a bad way the
chest of me is in tonight, Mammy. I think it's a little sleep I
should have now for meself. For there's mighty work in the
railyard tomorrow to be done. (*Pause*.) What's that,
Mammy? Me prayers? I know. Sure, would I be forgetting,
as well as you taught them to me? (*Blesses himself*.) And now I
lay me down to sleep, I pray to God my soul to keep. But if
. . . (*Pause*.) But if I die before I wake . . . I pray to God . . .
(*Tearfully*.) I pray to God . . .

Pause, recovering himself. He smiles.

Ara, don't worry, Mammy. 'Tis only to sleep it is that I'm going. 'Tis only to sleep.

Billy *lies down. His pained wheezes get worse and worse, until they suddenly stop with an anguished gasp, his eyes close, his head lolls to one side, and he lays there motionless. Fade to black.*

Scene Eight

A church hall in semi-darkness. **Bobby, Mammy** *(bottle in hand),* **Johnny, Helen, Bartley, Eileen** *and* **Kate** *sitting. All are staring up at the film* 'Man of Aran' *being projected. The film is nearing its end, and its soundtrack is either very low or not heard at all.*

Mammy   What's this that's happening?

Johnny   What does it look like that's happening?

Bartley   Aren't they going catching a shark, Mrs, and a big shark?

Mammy   Are they?

Johnny   Shut up and drink, you.

Mammy   I will, goosey.

Bobby   I hope only water it is that's in that bottle. Johnnypateenmike.

Johnny   Of course it's only water. (*Whispered.*) Don't be breathing out near Babbybobby, Mammy.

Mammy   I won't be.

Johnny   And mind the 'goosey'.

Bobby   Has your Johnny been thieving any more of your life savings lately, Mrs O'Dougal?

Johnny   I never ever thieved me mammy's life savings. I only borrowed them, short-term.

Mammy   Since 1914 this fecker's borrowed them short-term.

Johnny   Well that's me definition of short-term.

Kate (*pause*) That's a big fish.

Eileen 'Tis a shark, Kate.

Kate 'Tis a wha?

Eileen A shark, a shark!

Helen Have you forgot what a shark is, on top of talking to stones?

Bartley It's mostly off America you do get sharks, Mrs, and a host of sharks, and so close to shore sometimes they come, sure, you wouldn't even need a telescope to spot them, oh no . . .

Helen Oh telescopes, Jesus . . . !

Bartley It's rare that off Ireland you get sharks. This is the first shark I've ever seen off Ireland.

Johnny Ireland mustn't be such a bad place so if sharks want to come to Ireland.

Bartley (*pause*) Babbybobby, you weren't in long with the polis at all when you was took down for Johnnypat's head-stoning, how comes?

Bobby Oh the guard just laughed when he heard about Johnnypat's head-stoning. 'Use a brick next time,' he said. 'Stop piddling around with stones.'

Johnny That guard wants drumming out of the polis. Or at least to have spiteful rumours spread about him.

Bobby And we all know who the man for that job'll be.

Johnny He beats his wife with a poker, d'you know?

Helen Sure is that news? They don't let you in the polis *unless* you beat your wife with a poker.

Bobby And that's an outright lie anyways about the guard beating his wife with a poker. (*Pause.*) A biteen of a rubber hose was all he used.

Kate (*pause*) Not a word. Not a word from him.

Helen Is stony off again?

Eileen She is.

Helen   Hey, stony!

Eileen   Ar leave her, Helen, will ya?

Helen (*pause*)   Ah they're never going to be catching this fecking shark. A fecking hour they've been at it now, it seems like.

Bartley   Uh-huh. Three minutes would be more accurate.

Helen   If it was *me* had a role in this film the fecker wouldn't have lasted as long. One good clobber and we could all go home.

Bartley   One good clobber with Ray Darcy's axe, I suppose.

Helen   Cut the axe-talk, you.

Bartley   Doesn't shark-clobbering take a sight more effort than cat-besecting?

Johnny   What's this that Johnnypateen hears?

Helen grabs **Bartley** *by the hair and wrenches his head around as* **Johnny** *makes a note in a pocket book.*

Helen   Just you wait 'til I fecking get you home. Just you fecking wait . . .

Bartley   Ah that hurts, Helen, that hurts . . .

Helen   Of course it hurts. It's supposed to fecking hurt.

Bobby   Be leaving Bartley alone now, Helen.

Helen   Up your arse you, Babbybobby Bennett, you fecking kiss-reneger. Would *you* like to step outside with me?

Bobby   I wouldn't like to.

Helen   Shut your hole so.

Bobby   Not if there was to be kissing involved, anyways.

Helen *releases* **Bartley** *roughly.*

Johnny   A little noteen, now, Johnnypateen has made for himself. A side of lamb at minimum this news'll get me, off Patty Brennan or Jack Ellery anyways. Eheh.

Helen You'll be eating that lamb with a broken neck, so, if that news gets bandied about before Jack and Pat've paid up, ya feck.

Johnny Oh aye.

Bartley (*pause*) Look at the size of that fella's nose. (*Pause.*) Look at the size of that fella's nose I said.

Kate Have you been falling down any holes since, Bartley?

Bartley Oh Mrs, sure wasn't I seven when I fell down the bloody hole I fell down? D'ya have to keep dragging that up every year?

Helen (*pause*) Oh they still haven't caught this fecking shark! How hard is it?

<u>**Helen** *throws an egg at the screen.*</u>

Bobby Oh don't be pegging any more eggs at the film, Helen. Weren't the five you pegged at the poor woman in it enough?

Helen Not nearly enough. I never got her in the gob even once, the bitch. She keeps moving.

Bobby You'll ruin the egg-man's bedsheet anyways.

Helen Ah, the egg-man's bedsheet is used to being eggy.

Bartley How do you know the egg-man's bedsheets are used to being eggy, Helen?

Helen Em, Jim Finnegan's daughter was telling me.

Mammy (*pause*) Ah why don't they just leave the poor shark alone? He was doing no harm.

Johnny Sure what manner of a story would that be, leaving a shark alone! You want a dead shark.

Bobby A dead shark, aye, or a shark with no ears on him.

Johnny A dead shark, aye, or a shark kissed a green-teethed girl in Antrim.

Bobby Do you want a belt, you, mentioning green-teeth girls?

Johnny   Well you interrupted me and me mammy's shark debate.

Mammy   They should give the shark a belt, then leave the poor gosawer alone.

Johnny   Why are you in love with sharks all of a sudden? Wasn't it a shark ate daddy?

Mammy   It *was* a shark ate daddy, but Jaysus says you should forgive and forget.

Johnny   He doesn't say you should forgive and forget sharks.

Bartley *(pause)*   Sharks have no ears to begin with, anyways.

Pause. They look at him.

Babbybobby was saying a shark with no ears. (*Pause.*) Sharks have no ears to begin with, anyways.

Johnny   We've moved on from ears-talk, you, ya thick.

Bartley   What are we onto now?

Johnny   We're onto Jaysus forgiving sharks.

Bartley   Oh aye, that's an awful great topic for conversation.

Helen   I always preferred Pontius Pilate to Jesus. Jesus always seemed full of himself.

Bartley   Jesus drove a thousand pigs into the sea one time, did you ever hear tell of that story? Drowned the lot of the poor devils. They always seem to gloss o'er that one in school.

Kate   I didn't know Jesus could drive.

Helen   Mrs? You've gone loopy, haven't you, Mrs? Haven't you gone loopy?

Kate   I haven't gone loopy.

Helen   You have. Your stone was telling me earlier.

Kate   What did me stone say?

Helen   Did you hear that one, Bartley? 'What did me stone say?'

Johnny   Of course poor Kate's gone loopy, Helen, with the gosawer she raised and loved sixteen year preferring to take his TB to Hollywood for his dying than bear be in the company of her.

Eileen *stands with her hands to her head and turns to face* **Johnny**, *as does* **Bobby**.

Eileen (*stunned*)   Wha? Wha?

Johnny   Em, whoops.

Bobby *grabs* **Johnny** *roughly and drags him up*.

Bobby   Didn't I say to ya?! Didn't I say to ya?!

Johnny   Sure don't they have a right to know about their dying foster-babby, stabbed them in the back without a by-your-leave?

Bobby   Can't you keep anything to yourself?

Johnny   Johnnypateenmike was never a man for secrets.

Bobby   Outside with ya, so, and see if you can keep this beating a secret.

Johnny   You'll frighten me mammy, Babbybobby, you'll frighten me mammy . . .

Mammy   Ah you won't, Bobby. Go on and give him a good beating for yourself.

Johnny   That was the last omelette you'll ever eat in my house, ya bitch!

Mammy   Carrot omelettes don't go, anyways.

Johnny   You never like anything adventurous!

Johnny *is dragged off right by* **Bobby**. *Sound of his yelps getting more and more distant.* **Eileen** *is standing in front of* **Bartley**, *hands still to her head*.

Eileen   What was this Johnnypateen was saying about . . .

Bartley   Would you mind out of me way, Mrs, I can't see.

Eileen *moves over to* **Mammy**.

Helen   What's to fecking see anyways but more wet fellas with awful jumpers on them?

Eileen   Mrs O'Dougal, what now was this that your Johnny was saying?

Mammy (*pause*)   TB they say your Cripple Billy has, Eileen.

Eileen   No . . . !

Mammy   Or, they say he *had* anyways. Four months ago Billy was told, and told he had only three months left in him.

Bartley   That means he's probably been dead a month, Mrs. Simple subtraction that is. Three from four.

Eileen   Ah sure, if this is only your Johnnypateen's oul gossiping I wouldn't believe you at all . . .

Mammy   Aye, if it was Johnnypat's gossiping you wouldn't need to care a skitter about it, but Babbybobby's news this is. Cripple Billy showed him a letter from McSharry the night before they sailed. Sure, Babbybobby would never've taken Cripple Billy, only his heart went out to him. Didn't Bobby's Annie die of the same thing?

Eileen   She did, and in agony she died. Oh Cripple Billy. The days and nights I've cursed him for not writing us, when how could he write us at all?

Helen   When he was buried six feet under. Aye, that'd be an awful hard task.

Eileen   But . . . but Doctor McSharry five or six times I've asked, and nothing at all wrong with Billy did McSharry say there was.

Mammy   Sure, I suppose he was only trying not to hurt you Eileen, same as everyone around. (*Pause.*) I'm sorry, Eileen.

Helen *and* **Bartley** *stand and stretch, as the film ends.* **Eileen** *sits, tearfully.*

Helen   Oh thank Christ the fecker's over. A pile of fecking shite.

Bartley   And not a telescope in sight.

The film winds out, leaving the screen blank. A light goes on behind it, illuminating the silhouette of **Cripple Billy** *on the screen, which only* **Kate** *sees. She stands and stares at it.*

Mammy (*wheeling herself away*)   Did they catch the shark in the end, so, Helen?

Helen   Ah it wasn't even a shark at all, Mrs. It was a tall fella in a grey donkey jacket.

Mammy   How do you know, Helen?

Helen   Didn't I give the fella a couple of kisses to promise to put me in his next film, and didn't I stamp on the bollocks of him when his promise turned out untrue?

Mammy   All that fuss o'er a fella in a grey donkey jacket. I don't know.

Helen   He won't be playing any more sharks for a while anyways, Mrs, the stamp I gave the feck.

Helen *and* **Mammy** *exit.* **Bartley** *stands staring at* **Billy**'*s silhouette, having just spotted it.* **Eileen**, *crying, still has her back to it.* **Kate** *pulls back the sheet, revealing* **Billy**, *alive and well.*

Helen (*off. Calling out*)   Are you coming, you, fecker?

Bartley   In a minute I'm coming.

Billy   I didn't want to disturb ye 'til the film was o'er.

Eileen *turns, sees him, stunned.* **Kate** *drops her stone and embraces* **Billy**.

Bartley   Hello there, Cripple Billy.

Billy   Hello there, Bartley.

Bartley   Just back from America are ya?

Billy I am.

Bartley Uh-huh. (*Pause.*) Did you get me me Yalla-mallows?

Billy I didn't, Bartley.

Bartley Ar, ya fecking promised, Billy.

Billy They had only Fripple-Frapples.

Billy *tosses* **Bartley** *a packet of sweets.*

Bartley Ah jeebies, Fripple-Frapples'll do just as fine. Thank you, Cripple Billy.

Kate You're not dead at all, are you, Billy?

Billy I'm not, Aunty Kate.

Kate Well that's good.

Bartley What was it so, Billy? Did you write that doctor's letter yourself and only to fool Babbybobby into rowing ya, when there wasn't a single thing the matter with the health of you at all?

Billy I did, Bartley.

Bartley You're awful clever for a cripple-boy, Billy. Was it out of 'Biggles goes to Borneo' you got that idea? When Biggles tells the cannonball he has the measles so the cannonball won't eat Biggles at all?

Billy No, I made the idea up meself, Bartley.

Bartley Well now, it sounds awful similar, Billy.

Billy Well I made the idea up meself, Bartley.

Bartley Well you're even more clever than I thought you was so, Billy. You've made a laughing stock of every beggar on Inishmaan, all thought you'd gone and croaked it, like eejits, me included. Fair play to ya.

Eileen Not everyone on Inishmaan. Some us of only believed you'd run off, and run off because you couldn't stomach the sight of the ones who raised you.

Billy Not for a second was that true, Aunty Eileen, and wasn't the reason I returned that I couldn't bear to be parted from ye any longer? Didn't I take me screen test not a month ago and have the Yanks say to me the part was mine? But I had to tell them it was no go, no matter how much money they offered me, because I know now it isn't Hollywood that's the place for me. It's here on Inishmaan, with the people who love me, and the people I love back.

Kate *kisses him.*

Bartley Ireland can't be such a bad place, so, if cripple fellas turn down Hollywood to come to Ireland.

Billy To tell you the truth, Bartley, it wasn't an awful big thing at all to turn down Hollywood, with the arse-faced lines they had me reading for them. 'Can I not hear the wail of the banshees for me, as far as I am from me barren island home.'

Bartley *laughs.*

Billy 'An Irishman I am, begora! With a heart and a spirit on me not crushed be a hundred years of oppression. I'll be getting me shillelagh out next, wait'll you see'. A rake of shite. And had me singing the fecking 'Croppy Boy' then.

Kate Sure I think he'd make a great little actoreen, don't you, Eileen?

Bartley Them was funny lines, Cripple Billy. Do them again.

Kate I'll be off home and air your room out for you, Billy.

Bartley Em, you've forgot your stone, there, Mrs. Mighn't you want a chat on the way, now?

Kate Ah I'll leave me stone. I have me Billy-boy back now to talk to, don't I, Billy?

Billy You do, Aunty.

Kate *exits.*

Billy   Oh she hasn't started up with the bloody stones again, has she?

Bartley   She has. Talks to them day and night, and everybody laughs at her, me included.

Billy   You shouldn't laugh at other people's misfortunes, Bartley.

Bartley (*confused*)   Why?

Billy   I don't know why. Just that you shouldn't is all.

Bartley   But it's awful funny.

Billy   Even so.

Bartley   We-ell I disagree with you there, but you've got me me Fripple-Frapples so I won't argue the point. Will you tell me all about how great America is later, Cripple Billy?

Billy   I will, Bartley.

Bartley   Did you see any telescopes while you were over there?

Billy   I didn't.

Bartley (*disappointed*)   Oh. How about me Aunty Mary in Boston Massachusetts? Did you see her? She has funny brown hair on her.

Billy   I didn't, Bartley.

Bartley   Oh. (*Pause.*) Well, I'm glad you're not dead anyways, Cripple Billy.

Bartley *exits.*

Billy (*pause*)   That's all Bartley wants to hear is how great America is.

Eileen   Is it not so?

Billy   It's just the same as Ireland really. Full of fat women with beards.

Eileen *gets up, goes over to* **Billy** *and slaps him across the head.*

Billy   Aargh! What was that fer?!

Eileen   Forget fat women with beards! Would it have killed you to write a letter all the time you were away? No it wouldn't, and not a word. Not a blessed word!

Billy   Ah Aunty, I was awful busy.

Eileen   Uh-huh. Too busy to write your aunties, were worried sick about you, but not too busy to go buying Fripple-Frapples for an eejit gosawer and only to show off the big man you think you are.

Billy   Ah it only takes a minute to buy Fripple-Frapples, sure. Is that a fair comparison?

Eileen   Don't you go big-wording me when you know you're in the wrong.

Billy   Sure, 'Comparison' isn't a big word.

Eileen   Mr Yankee-high-and-mighty now I see it is.

Billy   And I found the American postal system awful complicated.

Eileen   It's any excuse for you. Well don't expect me to be forgiving and forgetting as quick as that one. She's only forgiven cos she's gone half doolally because of ya. You won't be catching me out so easy!

Billy   Ah don't be like that, Aunty.

Eileen (*exiting*)   I *will* be like that. I *will* be like that.

Long pause, **Billy***'s head lowered.* **Eileen** *sticks her head back in.*

And I suppose you'll be wanting praitie cakes for your tea too?!

Billy   I would, Aunty.

Eileen   Taahhh!

She exits again. Pause. **Billy** *looks at the sheet/screen, pulls it back across to its original dimensions and stands there staring at it, caressing it slightly, deep in thought.* **Bobby** *quietly enters right,* **Billy** *noticing him after a moment.*

Billy   Babbybobby. I daresay I owe you an explanation.

Bobby   There's no need to explain, Billy.

Billy   I want to, Bobby. See, I never thought at all this day would come when I'd have to explain. I'd hoped I'd disappear forever to America. And I would've too, if they'd wanted me there. If they'd wanted me for the filming. But they didn't want me. A blond lad from Fort Lauderdale they hired instead of me. He wasn't crippled at all, but the Yank said 'Ah, better to get a normal fella who can act crippled than a crippled fella who can't fecking act at all.' Except he said it ruder. (*Pause.*) I thought I'd done alright for meself with me acting. Hours I practised in me hotel there. And all for nothing. (*Pause.*) I gave it a go anyways. I had to give it a go. I had to get away from this place, Babbybobby, be any means, just like me mammy and daddy had to get away from this place. (*Pause.*) Going drowning meself I'd often think of when I was here, just to . . . just to end the laughing at me, and the sniping at me, and the life of nothing but shuffling to the doctor's and shuffling back from the doctor's and pawing over the same oul books and finding any other way to piss another day away. Another day of sniggering, or the patting me on the head like a broken-brained gosawer. The village orphan. The village cripple, and nothing more. Well, there are plenty round here just as crippled as me, only it isn't on the outside it shows. (*Pause.*) But the thing is, you're not one of them, Babbybobby, nor never were. You've a kind heart on you. I suppose that's why it was so easy to cod you with the TB letter, but that's why I was so sorry for codding you at the time and why I'm just as sorry now. Especially for codding you with the same thing your Mrs passed from. Just I thought that would be more effective. But, in the long run, I thought, or I hoped, that if you had a choice between you being codded a while and me doing away with meself, once your anger had died down anyways, you'd choose you being codded every time. Was I wrong, Babbybobby? Was I?

Bobby *slowly walks over to* **Billy**, *stops just in front of him, and lets a length of lead piping slide down his sleeve into his hand.*

Bobby   Aye.

Bobby *raises the pipe . . .*

Billy   No, Bobby, no . . . !

Billy *covers up as the pipe scythes down. Blackout, with the sounds of* **Billy***'s pained screams and the pipe scything down again and again.*

Scene Nine

The shop, late evening. The **Doctor** *tending to* **Billy***'s bruised and bloody face.* **Kate** *at the counter,* **Eileen** *at the door, looking out.*

Eileen   Johnnypateenmike's near enough running o'er the island with his news of Billy's return to us.

Kate   This is a big day for news.

Eileen   He has a loaf in one hand and a leg o' mutton neath each armeen.

Kate   Billy's return and Babbybobby's arrest and Jim Finnegan's daughter joining the nunnery then. That was the biggest surprise.

Eileen   The nuns must be after anybody if they let Jim Finnegan's daughter join them.

Kate   The nuns' standards must have dropped.

Billy   Sure why shouldn't Jim Finnegan's daughter become a nun? It's only pure gossip that Jim Finnegan's daughter is a slut.

Doctor   No, Jim Finnegan's daughter *is* a slut.

Billy   Is she?

Doctor   Aye.

Billy   How do you know?

Doctor   Just take me word.

Eileen   Isn't he a doctor?

Billy (*pause*)   Just I don't like people gossiping about
people is all. Haven't I had enough of that meself to last me a
lifetime?

Doctor   But aren't you the one who started half the
gossiping about you, with your forging of letters from me
you'll yet have to answer for?

Billy   I'm sorry about the letter business, Doctor, but
wasn't it the only avenue left open to me?

Eileen   It's 'Avenues' now, do ya hear?

Kate   It's always big-talk when from America they return.

Eileen   Avenues. I don't know.

Billy   Aunties, I think the doctor might be wanting a mug
of tea, would ye's both go and get him one?

Eileen   Is it getting rid of us you're after? If it is, just say so.

Billy   It's getting rid of ye I'm after.

Eileen *stares at him a moment then the two moodily exit to the back
room.*

Doctor   You shouldn't talk to them like that, now, Billy.

Billy   Ah they keep going on and on.

Doctor   I know they do but they're women.

Billy   I suppose. (*Pause.*) Would you tell me something,
Doctor? What do you remember of me mammy and daddy,
the people they were?

Doctor   Why do you ask?

Billy   Oh, just when I was in America there I often thought
of them, what they'd have done if they'd got there. Wasn't
that where they were heading the night they drowned?

Doctor   They say it was. (*Pause.*) As far as I can remember,
they weren't the nicest of people. Your daddy was an oul
drunken tough, would rarely take a break from his fighting.

Billy   I've heard me mammy was a beautiful woman.

Doctor   No, no, she was awful ugly.

Billy   Was she?

Doctor   Oh she'd scare a pig. But, ah, she seemed a pleasant enough woman, despite her looks, although the breath on her, well it would knock you.

Billy   They say it was that dad punched mammy while she was heavy with me was why I turned out the way I did.

Doctor   Disease caused you to turn out the way you did, Billy. Not punching at all. Don't go romanticising it.

Billy *coughs/wheezes slightly.*

Doctor   I see you still have your wheeze.

Billy   I still have a bit of me wheeze.

Doctor   That wheeze is taking a long time to go.

He uses a stethoscope to check **Billy**'*s chest.*

Has worse or better it got since your travelling? Breathe in.

Billy   Maybe a biteen worse.

The **Doctor** *listens to* **Billy**'*s back.*

Doctor   But blood you haven't been coughing up, ah no.

Billy   Ah a biteen of blood. (*Pause.*) Now and again.

Doctor   Breathe out. How often is now and again, Billy?

Billy (*pause*)   Most days. (*Pause.*) The TB is it?

Doctor   I'll have to be doing more tests.

Billy   But the TB it looks like?

Doctor   The TB it looks like.

Billy (*quietly*)   There's a coincidence.

Johnny *enters quietly, having been listening at the door, loaf in hand, a leg of lamb under each arm, which he carries throughout.*

Johnny   It's the TB after all?

Doctor   Oh Johnnypateen, will you ever stop listening at doors?

Johnny   Lord save us but from God I'm sure that TB was sent Cripple Billy, for claiming he had TB when he had no TB, and making Johnnypateen's news seem unreliable.

Doctor   God doesn't send people TB, Johnnypateen.

Johnny   He *does* send people TB.

Doctor   He doesn't, now.

Johnny   Well didn't he send the Egyptians boils is just as bad?

Doctor   Well boils is different from tuberculosis, Johnnypateen, and *no* he *didn't* send the Egyptians boils.

Johnny   In Egyptian times.

Doctor   No, he didn't.

Johnny   Well he did something to the fecking Egyptians!

Billy   He killed their first-born sons.

Johnny   He killed their first-born sons and dropped frogs on them, aye. There's a boy knows his scripture. Do your aunties know you have TB yet, Cripple Billy?

Billy   No, they don't know, and you're not to tell them.

Johnny   Sure it's me job to tell them!

Billy   It isn't your job at all to tell them, and don't you have enough news for one day. Can't you do me a favour for once in your life?

Johnny   For once in me life, is it? (*Sighing.*) Ah I won't tell them so.

Billy   Thank you, Johnnypateen.

Johnny   Johnnypateen's a kind-hearted, Christian man.

Doctor   I heard you were feeding your mammy poteen at the showing of the film today, Johnnypateen.

Johnny   I don't know where she got hold of that poteen. She's a devil, d'you know?

Doctor   Where's your mammy now?

Johnny   At home she is. (*Pause.*) Lying at the foot of me stairs.

Doctor   What's she doing lying at the foot of your stairs?

Johnny   Nothing. Just lying. Ah she seems happy enough. She has a pint with her.

Doctor   How did she *get* lying at the foot of your stairs?

Johnny   Be falling down them! How d'ya usually get lying at the foot of a fella's stairs?

Doctor   And you just left her there?

Johnny   Is it my job to go picking her up?

Doctor   It is!

Johnny   Sure, didn't I have work to do with me news-divulging? I have better things to do than picking mammies up. D'you see the two legs of lamb I got, and a loafeen too? This is a great day.

The **Doctor** *packs up his black bag, stunned, as* **Johnny** *admires his meat.*

Doctor   I'm off now, Billy, to Johnnypateen's house, to see if his mammy's dead or alive. Will you come see me tomorrow, for those further tests?

Billy   I will, Doctor.

The **Doctor** *exits, staring at* **Johnny** *all the way.* **Johnny** *sits down beside* **Billy**.

Johnny   Me mammy isn't lying at the foot of me stairs at all. It's just I can't stand the company of that boring feck.

Billy   That wasn't a nice thing to do, Johnnypateen.

Johnny   Well you're hardly the world's authority on nice things to do, now, are you, Cripple Billy?

Billy   I'm not at that, I suppose.

Johnny   Ah what harm? Do what you want and feck everybody else is Johnnypateenmichael's motto.

Billy   Did you hear McSharry talking about my mammy when you were listening at the door?

Johnny   A bit of it.

Billy   Was he accurate about her?

Johnny *shrugs*.

Billy   Oh isn't it always on this subject your lips stay sealed, yet on every other subject from feuds o'er geese to ewe-maiming be lonely fellas, your lips go flapping like a cabbage in the breeze?

Johnny   Now, on the subject of feuds over geese, have you heard the latest?

Billy *sighs*.

Johnny   Well we all thought Jack Ellery and Patty Brennan were apt to go killing each other o'er the slaughter of their cat and their goose, but now d'you know what? A child seen them, just this morning there, kissing the faces off each other in a haybarn. I can't make it out for the life of me. Two fellas kissing, and two fellas who don't even like each other.

Billy (*pause*)   You've changed the subject, Johnnypateen.

Johnny   I'm great at changing subjects, me. What was the subject? Oh, your drowned mammy and daddy.

Billy   Were they gets like McSharry says?

Johnny   They weren't at all gets.

Billy   No? And yet they still left me behind when they sailed off.

Eileen *returns with mug of tea*.

Eileen   I've the Doctor's tea.

Billy   The Doctor's gone.

Eileen   Without having his tea?

Billy   Evidently.

Eileen Don't you be big-wording me again, Billy Claven.

Johnny I'll have the Doctor's tea so, if it'll save a family dispute.

She gives him the tea.

Johnnypateen goes out of his way to help people out, and do you have any biscuits there, Mrs?

Billy You're changing the subject again, aren't ya?

Johnny I'm not changing the subject. I want a biscuit.

Eileen We have no biscuits.

Johnny I'll bet you have a rake of biscuits. What do you have on the shelves behind them peas, there?

Eileen We have more peas.

Johnny You order too many peas. A fella can't go having peas with his tea. Unless he was an odd fella. (*Adjusting lamb.*) And there's no way you could describe Johnnypateenmike as an odd fella. Oh no.

Billy Johnnypateen. Me mammy and daddy. Their sailing.

Eileen Oh that's ancient news, Billy. Just leave it alone . . .

Johnny Sure if the boy wants to hear, let him hear. Isn't he grown up and travelled enough now to be hearing?

Eileen You're not going telling him?

Johnny stares at her a moment.

Johnny It was on the sands I met them that night, staring off into the black, the water roaring, and I wouldn't've thought a single thing more of it, if I hadn't seen the sack full of stones tied to the hands of them there, as they heaved it into the boat. A big old hemp sack like one of them there, it was. And they handed you to me then, then started rowing, to deep water.

Billy So they *did* kill themselves o'er me?

Johnny They killed themselves, aye, but not for the reasons you think. D'you think it was to get away from ya?

Billy Why else, sure?

Johnny Will I tell him?

Eileen *nods.*

Johnny A week before this it was they'd first been told you'd be dying if they couldn't get you to the Regional Hospital and medicines down you. But a hundred pounds or near this treatment'd cost. They didn't have the like of a hundred pounds. I know you know it was their death insurance paid for the treatment saved you. But did you know it was the same day I met them on the sands there they had taken their insurance policy out.

Billy (*pause*)   It was for me they killed themselves?

Johnny The insurance paid up a week after, and you were given the all-clear afore a month was out.

Billy So they *did* love me, in spite of everything.

Eileen They did love you *because* of everything, Billy.

Johnny Isn't that news?

Billy That is news. I needed good news this day. Thank you, Johnnypateen.

They shake hands and **Billy** *sits.*

Johnny You're welcome, Cripple Billy.

Billy *Billy.*

Johnny Billy. (*Pause.*) Well, I'm off home to me mammy. Hopefully she'll have dropped down dead when the Doctor barged in and we'll both have had good news this day. (*Pause.*) Mrs, d'you have any payment there for Johnnypateen's good news and not peas?

Eileen There's Yalla-mallows.

Johnny (*looking at packet*)   What are Yalla-mallows?

Eileen They're mallows that are yalla.

Johnny (*pause. After considering*)   I'll leave them.

Johnny *exits. Long pause.*

Billy   You should have told me before, Aunty.

Eileen   I wasn't sure how you'd take the news, Billy.

Billy   You still should've told me. The truth is always less hard than you fear it's going to be.

Eileen   I'm sorry, Billy.

Pause. **Billy** *lets her cuddle him slightly.*

Billy   And I'm sorry for using 'Evidently' on ya.

Eileen   And so you should be.

She gently slaps his face, smiling. **Helen** *enters.*

Hello, Helen. What can I get you?

Helen   No, I've just come to look at Cripple Billy's wounds. I've heard they're deep.

Billy   Hello, Helen.

Helen   You look a fecking fool in all that get-up, Cripple Billy.

Billy   I do, I suppose. Em, Aunty, is that the kettle, now, I hear boiling in the back?

Eileen   Eh? No. Oh. (*Tuts.*) Aye.

Eileen *exits to back room, as* **Helen** *pulls up* **Billy**'s *bandages to look under them.*

Billy   Hurts a bit that picking does, Helen.

Helen   Ar don't be such a fecking girl, Cripple Billy. How was America?

Billy   Fine, fine.

Helen   Did you see any girls over there as pretty as me?

Billy   Not a one.

Helen   Or almost as pretty as me?

Billy   Not a one.

Helen   Or even a hundred times *less* pretty than me?

Billy   Well, maybe a couple, now.

Helen *pokes him hard in the face.*

Billy (*in pain*)   Aargh! Not a one, I mean.

Helen   You just watch yourself you, Cripple Billy.

Billy   Do ya have to be so violent, Helen?

Helen   I do have to be so violent, or if I'm not to be taken advantage of anyways I have to be so violent.

Billy   Sure, nobody's taken advantage of you since the age of seven, Helen.

Helen   Six is nearer the mark. I ruptured a curate at six.

Billy   So couldn't you tone down a bit of your violence and be more of a sweet girl?

Helen   I could, you're right there. And the day after I could shove a bent spike up me arse. (*Pause.*) I've just lost me job with the egg-man.

Billy   Why did you lose your job with the egg-man, Helen?

Helen   D'you know, I can't for the life of me figure out why. Maybe it was me lack of punctuality. Or me breaking all the egg-man's eggs. Or me giving him a good kick whenever I felt like it. But you couldn't call them decent reasons.

Billy   You couldn't at all, sure.

Helen   Or me spitting on the egg-man's wife, but you couldn't call that a decent reason.

Billy   What did you spit on the egg-man's wife for, Helen?

Helen   Ah the egg-man's wife just deserves spitting on. (*Pause.*) I still haven't given you a good kick for your taking your place in Hollywood that was rightfully mine. Didn't I have to kiss four of the film directors on Inishmore to book me place you took without a single kiss?

Billy But there was only *one* film director on Inishmore that time, Helen. The man Flaherty. And I didn't see you near him at all.

Helen Who was it I was kissing so?

Billy I think it was mostly stable-boys who could do an American accent.

Helen The bastards! Couldn't you've warned me?

Billy I was going to warn you, but you seemed to be enjoying yourself.

Helen You do get a decent kiss off a stable-boy, is true enough. I would probably go stepping out with a stable-boy if truth be told, if it wasn't for the smell of pig-shite you get off them.

Billy Are you not stepping out with anyone at the moment, so?

Helen I'm not.

Billy (*pause*)   Me, I've never been kissed.

Helen Of course you've never been kissed. You're a funny-looking cripple-boy.

Billy (*pause*)   It's funny, but when I was in America I tried to think of all the things I'd miss about home if I had to stay in America. Would I miss the scenery, I thought? The stone walls, and the lanes, and the green, and the sea? No, I wouldn't miss them. Would I miss the food? The peas, the praities, the peas, the praities and the peas? No, I wouldn't miss it. Would I miss the people?

Helen Is this speech going to go on for more long?

Billy I've nearly finished it. (*Pause.*) What was me last bit? You've put me off . . .

Helen 'Would I miss the people.'

Billy Would I miss the people? Well, I'd miss me aunties, or a *bit* I'd miss me aunties. I wouldn't miss Babbybobby with his lead stick or Johnnypateen with his daft news. Or all the lads used to laugh at me at school, or all the lasses used to cry if I even spoke to them. Thinking over it, if Inishmaan sank in the sea tomorrow, and everybody on it up and drowned, there isn't especially anybody I'd really miss. Anybody other than you, that is, Helen.

Helen (*pause*)   You'd miss the cows you go staring at.

Billy   Oh that cow business was blown up out of all proportion. What I was trying to build up to, Helen, was . . .

Helen   Oh, was you trying to build up to something, Cripple Billy?

Billy   I was, but you keep interrupting me.

Helen   Build up ahead so.

Billy   I was trying to build up to . . . There comes a time in every fella's life when he has to take his heart in his hands and make a try for something, and even though he knows it's a one in a million chance of him getting it, he has to chance it still, else why be alive at all? So, I was wondering Helen, if maybe sometime, y'know, when you're not too busy or something, if maybe . . . and I know well I'm no great shakes to look at, but I was wondering if maybe you might want to go out walking with me some evening. Y'know, in a week or two or something?

Helen (*pause*)   Sure what would I want to go out walking with a cripple-boy for? It isn't out walking you'd be anyways, it would be out shuffling, because you can't walk. I'd have to be waiting for ya every five yards. What would you and me want to be out shuffling for?

Billy   For the company.

Helen   For the company?

Billy   And . . .

Helen   And what?

Billy   And for the way sweethearts be.

Helen *looks at him a second, then slowly and quietly starts laughing/ sniggering through her nose, as she gets up and goes to the door. Once there she turns, looks at* **Billy** *again, laughs again and exits.* **Billy** *is left staring down at the floor as* **Kate** *quietly enters from the back room.*

Kate   She's not a very nice girl anyways, Billy.

Billy   Was you listening, Aunty Kate?

Kate   I wasn't listening or alright I was a biteen listening. (*Pause.*) You wait for a nice girl to come along, Billy. A girl who doesn't mind at all what you look like. Just sees your heart.

Billy   How long will I be waiting for a girl like that to come along, Aunty?

Kate   Ah not long at all, Billy. Maybe a year or two. Or at the outside five.

Billy   Five years . . .

Billy *nods, gets up, wheezes slightly, and exits into the back room.* **Kate** *starts tidying and closing up the shop.* **Eileen** *enters, helping her. Sound of* **Billy** *coughing distantly in the house now and then.*

Eileen   What's Cripple Billy looking so glum for?

Kate   Billy asked Slippy Helen to go out walking with him, and Helen said she'd rather go out walking with a broken-headed ape.

Eileen   That was a descriptive turn of phrase for Slippy Helen.

Kate   Well, I've tarted it up a bit.

Eileen   I was thinking. (*Pause.*) Cripple Billy wants to aim lower than Helen, really.

Kate   Cripple Billy *does* want to aim lower than Helen.

Eileen   Billy wants to aim at ugly girls who are thick, then work his way up.

Kate   Billy should go to Antrim really. He'd be well away. (*Pause.*) But Billy probably doesn't like ugly girls who are thick.

Eileen Sure there's no pleasing Billy.

Kate None.

Eileen (*pause*) And you missed the story Johnnypateen spun, Kate, about Billy's mam and daddy tying a sack of stones to their hands and drowning themselves for their insurance money that saved him.

Kate The stories Johnnypateen spins. When it was poor Billy they tied in that sack of stones, and Billy would still be at the bottom of the sea to this day, if it hadn't been for Johnnypateen swimming out to save him. And stealing his mammy's hundred pounds then to pay for Billy's hospital treatment.

Eileen We should tell Billy the true story some day, Kate.

Kate Sure, that story might only make Cripple Billy sad, or something, Eileen.

Eileen Do you think? Ah there's plenty of time to tell Billy that story anyways.

Kate There is.

The two finish their closing up, **Eileen** *locking the door,* **Kate** *turning the oil lamp low.*

This'll be the first decent night's sleep in many a month I've had, Eileen.

Eileen I know it will, Kate. Have you finished for good with your stone shenanigans now?

Kate I *have*. They only crop up when I've been worrying, and, you know, I know I hide it well, but I do worry awful about Billy when he's away from us.

Eileen I do worry awful about Billy when he's away from us too, but I try not to let stones enter into it.

Kate Ah let's forget about stones. We have our Billy back with us now.

Eileen We *do* have our Billy back with us. Back for good.

Kate Back for good.

The two smile and exit to the back room, arm-in-arm. After a pause, **Billy** *comes in from the back, sniffling, and turns the oil lamp up, revealing his bloodshot eyes and tear-stained cheeks. He quietly takes the sack down from the wall, places inside it numerous cans of peas until it's very heavy, then ties the cords at the top of the bag tightly around one of his hands. This done, he pauses in thought a moment, then shuffles to the door. There is a knock on it.* **Billy** *dries his cheeks, hides the sack behind him and opens the door.* **Helen** *pops her head in.*

Helen (*forcefully*)   All right so I'll go out walking with ya, but only somewheres no fecker would see us and when it's dark and no kissing or groping, cos I don't want you ruining me fecking reputation.

Billy   Oh. Okay, Helen.

Helen   Or anyways not much kissing or groping.

Billy   Would tomorrow suit?

Helen   Tomorrow wouldn't at all suit. Isn't it Bartley's fecking birthday tomorrow?

Billy   Is it? What have you got him?

Helen   I got him . . . and for the life of me I don't know why I did because I know now he'll never stop fecking jabbering on about it or anyways won't stop jabbering 'til I give him a big thump in the fecking face for himself and even then he probably won't stop, but didn't I get the fecker a telescope?

Billy   That was awful nice of ya, Helen.

Helen   I think I must be getting soft in me old age.

Billy   I think so too.

Helen   Do ya?

Billy   Aye.

Helen (*coyly*)   Do ya really, Billy?

Billy   I do.

Helen   Uh-huh. Does this feel soft?

Helen *pokes* **Billy** *hard in the bandaged face.* **Billy** *yelps in pain.*

Billy   Aargh! No, it doesn't feel soft!

Helen   Good-oh. I'll see you the day after tomorrow for our fecking walk, so.

Billy   You will.

Helen *kisses* **Billy** *briefly, winks at him, and pulls the door behind her as she exits.* **Billy** *is left standing there stunned a moment, then remembers the sack tied to his hand. Pause. He unties it, replaces the cans on the shelves and hangs the sack back up on the wall, stroking it a moment. He shuffles over towards the back room, smiling, but stops as he gets there, coughing heavily, his hand to his mouth. After the coughing stops he takes his hand away and looks down at it for a moment. It's covered in blood.* **Billy** *loses his smile, turns the oil lamp down and exits to the back room. Fade to black.*

Methuen Modern Plays

include work by

Jean Anouilh	John McGrath
John Arden	David Mamet
Margaretta D'Arcy	Patrick Marber
Peter Barnes	Arthur Miller
Sebastian Barry	Mtwa, Ngema & Simon
Brendan Behan	Tom Murphy
Edward Bond	Phyllis Nagy
Bertolt Brecht	Peter Nichols
Howard Brenton	Joseph O'Connor
Simon Burke	Joe Orton
Jim Cartwright	Louise Page
Caryl Churchill	Joe Penhall
Noël Coward	Luigi Pirandello
Sarah Daniels	Stephen Poliakoff
Nick Dear	Franca Rame
Shelagh Delaney	Philip Ridley
David Edgar	Reginald Rose
Dario Fo	David Rudkin
Michael Frayn	Willy Russell
John Godber	Jean-Paul Sartre
Paul Godfrey	Sam Shepard
John Guare	Wole Soyinka
Peter Handke	C. P. Taylor
Jonathan Harvey	Theatre de Complicite
Iain Heggie	Theatre Workshop
Declan Hughes	Sue Townsend
Terry Johnson	Judy Upton
Barrie Keeffe	Timberlake Wertenbaker
Stephen Lowe	Victoria Wood
Doug Lucie	

Methuen World Classics

Aeschylus (two volumes)
Jean Anouilh
John Arden (two volumes)
Arden & D'Arcy
Aristophanes (two volumes)
Aristophanes & Menander
Brendan Behan
Aphra Behn
Edward Bond (four volumes)
Bertolt Brecht
 (five volumes)
Büchner
Bulgakov
Calderón
Anton Chekhov
Noël Coward (five volumes)
Sarah Daniels (two volumes)
Eduardo De Filippo
David Edgar (three volumes)
Euripides (three volumes)
Dario Fo (two volumes)
Michael Frayn (two volumes)
Max Frisch
Gorky
Harley Granville Barker
 (two volumes)
Henrik Ibsen (six volumes)
Terry Johnson
Lorca (three volumes)

Marivaux
Mustapha Matura
David Mercer (two volumes)
Arthur Miller
 (five volumes)
Anthony Minghella
Molière
Tom Murphy
 (three volumes)
Musset
Peter Nichols (two volumes)
Clifford Odets
Joe Orton
Louise Page
A. W. Pinero
Luigi Pirandello
Stephen Poliakoff
 (two volumes)
Terence Rattigan
Ntozake Shange
Sophocles (two volumes)
Wole Soyinka
David Storey (two volumes)
August Strindberg
 (three volumes)
J. M. Synge
Ramón del Valle-Inclán
Frank Wedekind
Oscar Wilde